The
Christening
of KARMA

Books by Geddes MacGregor

Apostles Extraordinary (*to be released in 1984*)
Reincarnation as a Christian Hope
The Gospels as a Mandala of Wisdom (Quest)
The Nicene Creed
Scotland Forever Home
Gnosis (Quest)
Reincarnation in Christianity (Quest)
He Who Lets Us Be
The Rhythm of God
Philosophical Issues in Religious Thought
So Help Me God
A Literary History of the Bible
The Sense of Absence
God Beyond Doubt
The Hemlock and the Cross
The Coming Reformation
Introduction to Religious Philosophy
The Bible in the Making
Corpus Christi
The Thundering Scot
The Vatican Revolution
The Tichborne Imposter
From a Christian Ghetto
Les Frontieres de la morale et de la religion
Christian Doubt
Aesthetic Experience in Religion

Cover art by *Jane A. Evans*

The Christening of KARMA

The Secret of Evolution

GEDDES MacGREGOR

*This publication made possible with
the assistance of the Kern Foundation*

THE THEOSOPHICAL PUBLISHING HOUSE
Wheaton, Ill. U.S.A. / Madras, India / London, England

The Theosophical Publishing House
306 West Geneva Road
Wheaton, Illinois 60189

Published by The Theosophical Publishing House, a department of The Theosophical Society in America.

Library of Congress Cataloging in Publication Data
MacGregor, Geddes.
    The christening of karma.

    (A Quest book)
    "A Quest original."
    Includes index.
    1. Karma. 2. Evolution. 3. Theosophy. I. Title.
BP573.K3M33   1984   291.2'2   83-40234
ISBN 0-8356-0581-7 (pbk.)

Printed in the United States of America

Contents

1

Evolution and Karma

Evolution is not a force but a process; not a cause but a law.

John Morley, *On Compromise*

What avails it to fight with the eternal laws of mind, which adjust the relation of all persons to each other, by the mathematical measure of their havings and beings?

Emerson, *Spiritual Laws*

In the course of my teaching and lecturing in universities and other institutions, I have discovered during the past decade or more an increasing interest in the concept of karma. It comes out in discussion at the slightest provocation and indeed sometimes with no detectable provocation at all. It is not always well understood. Too often it is so ill understood as to be taken for a kind of fatalism, which it certainly is not, being on the contrary a freewill doctrine, although it is much else besides. Yet, understood well or badly, it commands a lively interest, not least on the part of young people who twenty years ago would not have generally found it so challenging to their outlook on life.

The connection of karma with evolutionary thought is not by any means always immediately apparent to those whom the concept of karma so fascinates. Yet the connection is crucial if karma is to be seen as a deeply spiritual principle at the heart of all things. To those who understand and accept the karmic principle, biological evolution, as Darwin and others have expounded it, is only a pointer to a far more

1

fundamental evolutionary principle in the very mind of God. Most Christians, though by no means all, have come to see no incompatibility between biological evolution and the Bible. Many, however, see the karmic principle as alien to both the Bible and the Church. True, the Sanskrit word *karma* is unfamiliar, but the concept, as we shall abundantly see, is at the root of the Judaeo-Christian tradition. I wish to argue, in this book that evolution and karma can be christened at the same font. Nor will they have been the first heretical-sounding ideas to have been so received.

The Christian Church's debt to heretics is incalculably great. The theory of Nicholas Copernicus (1473-1543), the father of modern astronomy, that the sun does not move round the earth but the earth round the sun, was supported by the investigations of Galileo Galilei (1564-1642). In February 1616 the consulting theologians of Rome's Holy Office condemned the Copernican theory as heretical, since it appeared to be incompatible with certain biblical passages that refer to the sun's rising and setting and even to the sun's having stood still for a brief period at Joshua's command (Joshua 10.12-14). Shortly after this ecclesiastical condemnation, Galileo was ordered not "to hold, teach or defend" the condemned proposition that the earth moves round the sun. For some years Galileo remained silent on the subject , but eventually the publication of his now famous *Dialogo* in 1630 led to his being handed over to the Inquisition in 1633 and, under threat of torture, forced to recant. He was condemned to imprisonment but released after some months and allowed to return home to Florence. The ban on the Copernican theory, which had caused the work of Copernicus to be put on the Index of Prohibited Books (that is, books that the faithful are not permitted to read without specific permission) was not removed till 1787, eleven years after the American Declaration of Independence.

Surely no one today would see the now well-established view that the sun is at the center of the solar system and that the earth moves in orbit round it as in any way irreconcilable to the Bible or in any sense detrimental either to the Christian or to any other religious faith. Not even the most literalistic of Bible readers would find any ground for resisting the acceptance of this basic tenet of modern astronomy or indeed see any need to oppose it in the interest of protecting or defending religious faith. On the contrary it is a view that is taken for granted as much by believers as by unbelievers. I know of no one with even the most elementary knowledge of astronomy who would feel the slightest need to disown this basic astronomical view as incompatible with anything in the Bible. Most educated believers, indeed, would see this along with much else in modern astronomy as intensifying and enriching their religious faith rather than in any way threatening or impoverishing it.

The "natural" sciences (physics, chemistry, biology, for example) are by no means a threat to religious truth. In the Middle Ages, when the Arab world was the focus of much scientific and mathematical inquiry and discovery, the truths disclosed seemed at first sight incompatible with the teaching of Islam as set forth in the Qur'ān. When, in the twelfth century, the discovery of Aristotle who represented "science" to the medieval Christian mind, alarmed churchmen, the prospect of reconciling him with the Bible looked at first dim indeed. In the following century, however, Thomas Aquinas not only reconciled much of Aristotle's science with the Bible and the teaching of the Church but showed with skill and brilliance that Aristotelianism enhanced rather than diminished the spirituality of the Church's treasure house. The marriage of "science and religion" in Thomas's work was eminently successful in terms of his day. Although of course enormous advances have been made since then, both in scientific investigation and in understanding and appreciation of the message of the Bible and the teaching of the Church, scholars now recognize the immense philosophical and theological acumen of Thomas and other medieval schoolmen and the light they shed on the intellectual problems of their time. They are no more to be despised for it (as for some centuries they were) than Christopher Columbus is to be disdained for having used the *Santa Maria* rather than a fast liner or a jumbo jet to cross the Atlantic.

From the standpoint of a modern scientist, one of the most obvious handicaps of medieval thinkers such as Thomas Aquinas and Duns Scotus is that they knew nothing about biological evolution. This did not merely obscure to them one or another aspect of the range of the knowledge we have today; it distorted their knowledge at a level so radical that their ignorance of it affected virtually everything in their thought. When we go on to reflect that until the speculations of Kant in his *General Natural History of the Heavens*, published in 1755, not only religious people but scientists with no religious axe to grind, took a very static view of the universe around them. Archbishop James Ussher (1581-1656), as is well known, fixed the date of the creation of the world at the year 4004 B.C. John Lightfoot (1602-1675) improved on this dating, having worked out not only the exact day but the hour: Friday, October 23, at 9 a.m. Even the great Isaac Newton (1642-1727), however, although he did propose in a private letter that the solar system could have evolved from a more primitive distribution of matter, seemed to see no need to pursue any such hypothesis. Kant was the first thinker to take the idea of cosmic evolution seriously; but his work on this subject attracted little attention. Pierre Simon, Marquis de Laplace, in his *Exposition du système du monde*, published in 1796, proposed the nebular hypothesis, and other scientists suggested various theories that also implied some sort of evolutionary notion. The Scottish Lord Monboddo (1714-1799) in his *The Origin and Progress of Language*, published in 1773, entertained a remarkably interesting evolutionary speculation that brought man into the same species as the orang-outang; but his work on this subject found little or no acceptance among his contemporaries. Among biologists, Jean-Baptiste de Monet, the Chevalier de Lamarck (1744-1829), may be accounted the first to take a clearly evolutionary view of the origin of man. His work was overshadowed by that of Charles Darwin, whose extremely influential book, *The Origin of Species*, published in 1859, soon revolutionized biological thought throughout the civilized world.

Opposition to Darwin came swiftly and bearing a religious banner. At a meeting of the British Association on June 30, 1860, the Bishop of Oxford, Samuel Wilberforce, whose persuasive oratory had earned for him the nickname "Soapy Sam," attacked it in the name of Christianity. That now notorious incident occurred some sixty-five years before the now even more notorious Scopes trial in Tennessee.

As time went on, however, thoughtful believers began to see that evolution could mean far more than having a simian ancestry and repudiating the literal interpretation of the Genesis account of creation as a six-day *opus*. They saw, too, that although Darwin, as a scientist, simply reported his findings and that these findings *suggested* the lack of any divine activity in the process of evolution, there was no more reason to repudiate religious belief on account of Darwin than there had been to reject it some centuries earlier on account of Galileo.

The Darwinians were properly concerned only with biological evolution; but what if there be a process of spiritual evolution that requires biological evolution as its antecedent? That is precisely what many discovered, having used the Darwinian theory as a catalyst for the discovery. Evolutionism so molded late nineteenth-century thought as to make it impossible for any well-educated person to avoid its all-pervasive influence.

What practical difference does it make in our daily lives now? That is almost like asking what difference it makes to see the earth in orbit round the sun rather than the reverse, as in the geocentric theory once very widely held. What difference does it make to know, as we now do, that the solar system itself is but an out-of-the way backwater in the indescribably immense universe? What people know about quantum physics and the theory of relativity, even at the most popular level, affects them at every point. Even though a person spend a whole lifetime between a little room and the village store below it, such knowledge transforms the entire outlook of that person, transmogrifying the quality of his or her daily living.

An understanding and appreciation of the evolutionary principle, however, affects me even more intimately and personally, because it so directly concerns the existential situation in which I find myself: my origin and my final destiny as well as the why of my being here right now. If evolution is both biological and spiritual, I am in the midst of a divine process directly touching me and all around me. I become an agent in the process, not a mere puppet in a divine drama.

Far more than all that: evolution directly affects my personal destiny, for I can now see *myself* as evolving. I am growing, developing. Not only does this attune me to the growth and development of plants and animals around me; it attunes me to the divine activity within me and encompassing me. Above all I become aware of the possibility of my making a qualitative "vertical leap" that will raise my consciousness to startlingly higher levels of awareness. Moreover, I can see such sudden spurts of spiritual advancement in my past. Finally, and by no means least, I can see more clearly the dangers that attend spiritual advancement and the steps that must be taken to avert these dangers. Besides, I recognize that nothing in all this requires me to renounce anything of spiritual value contained in what I have ever accepted as God's revealing or unfolding of himself to me. I see both how far I have come and how far I have to go and above all the importance of all that I do here and now. Indeed, whereas I had been a mere passenger in a bus, now I am flying my own plane.

Of course it is possible to restrict evolution to the life process in a naturalistic way, ignoring or repudiating moral and spiritual dimensions as mere dreams of the human brain. Recognition of the evolutionary process does not in itself force us into a religious or an irreligious stance, into belief or unbelief in this or that religious affirmation. What I shall try to show in this book is that an evolutionary understanding of the universe, including ourselves, immensely enlivens and deepens whatever disposition to religious belief we may be willing to entertain and whatever spiritual perception we may in any case enjoy. This, I shall contend, is true irrespective of the way in which we may symbolize God; that is to say, it works for Parsee as for Buddhist, for Muslim as for Hindu, for Christian as for Jew. Since I am writing primarily for people whose roots lie in the West and whose thinking is therefore in a Western mold, my examples will be often from Christian thought and experience; but this should not obscure the universality of the principle I seek to establish.

In some religious circles today it is fashionable to set creation and evolution each in opposition to the other as though the one excluded the other. On the contrary, on the view I am to present, the creative process is evolutionary in the sense that it is the way God does things, and evolution is creationist in the sense that it is eternally governed by the heart and mind of God who is at the core of all things, being (as Aristotle in his own way saw long ago) the eternal principle that like a magnet draws all things to itself. By recognizing the evolutionary character of all things, we can be led to perceive that that principle is both suprapersonal and supra-impersonal, both far beyond our ken "in light inaccessible" and permeating all things to their uttermost edges, setting the Kingdom of God indeed within us.

The notion that evolution sets "science" at enmity with "religion" is a conspicuously misguided view. Those whose fears lead them to canvass it show in doing so that they do not know their foes from their friends. An evolutionary interpretation of the universe such as modern physicists, astronomers, and biologists find themselves compelled to make in face of the evidence confronting them sits much better with a view such as the traditional Judaeo-Christian one than a "static," non-evolutionary one. For if we found the universe to be *not* evolutionary but "static," we could find it much easier to interpret as simply and inexplicably eternally *there* with no need of a divine Being either behind it or within it or both to sustain and order it. It could not be otherwise than it is, and so the famous question posed by Leibniz in the seventeenth century and by Heidegger in the twentieth, "Why is there anything at all and not just nothing?" would be indeed a pointless if not meaningless question. If, however, the universe is evolutionary as the basic modern sciences show it to be, then it is much more plausible to say that it is as it is not by necessity but by some sort of decision or choice. Of course this certainly does not "prove" that there is a divine Being behind and/or within it; but no less certainly does it make such a view at least possible and to some even probable. Furthermore, if you do take the view that God is behind and/or within the universe, you will find it eminently congenial to go on to perceive him as freely choosing to have the universe the way it happens to be rather than as a static entity somehow existing of necessity. So while surely no one with any philosophical training and scientific understanding at all would pretend that the principle of evolution leads inevitably to the view that God is behind and/or within it, evolution should most emphatically never be deemed by any educated person to be something that religious people should attack as hostile to religious belief.

The ancient concept of karma fits so well into a general evolutionary understanding of the universe that it may be considered the "law" underlying any spiritual interpretation of the evolutionary process. Those in the ancient world who understood it as it was generally presented in Indian thought did not know, of course, of biological evolution in terms such as have been used in the exposition of Darwinian theory. Yet in their own way they did see an evolutionary principle at work; hence their sense of the continuity of human with lower forms of life and their reverence for life in all its forms. When, in the nineteenth century, the scientific community was convinced of the fundamental truth of Darwin's theory of evolution, a renaissance among religious-minded people of the notion of the karmic principle was to be expected. We find it appearing in a variety of forms in European and American literature. In the last quarter of that century, after the foundation of the Theosophical Society in 1875, interest in karma was further developed.

Karma, as we shall see over and over again in the course of our present study, is inseparable from the spiritual side of the evolutionary coin. It is the principle of evolution understood in specifically moral terms. While its workings extend to all stages of development, its effect on our personal lives can be seen ever more clearly as we advance in spirituality. Karma is much more than a principle of justice, although it includes that as one of its many aspects. It is a principle of harmony and reason and love at the heart of all things. It manifests itself to us in many ways, not least in our personal endowments and capabilities as well as in our personal circumstances. From its workings is derived, for example, the temperament with which we are born as well as the love or lovelessness with which we find ourselves surrounded in our formative years. In the thought of those who see themselves as pilgrims on a spiritual path, karma and evolution go together as two halves of the same scissors.

Since the primary focus of our concern in this book is to consider how concepts such as evolution and karma can be legitimately reconciled to Christianity, we must deal with an obvious objection before we go any further. The objection may be stated as follows: what warrant can possibly be found in the Bible, which all Christians, in one way or another, recognize as the primary documents of their faith? In the absence of such a warrant, how can anyone dare to propose the christening of such ideas?

Certainly one would look in vain in the Bible for an evolutionary understanding of the universe, either in physical, biological, or any other terms. Likewise, the doctrine of karma (although, as we shall see, it is often implied) is not to be found expressly stated as such in the Bible. No chapter-and-verse authority for the christening of karma and evolution could ever be provided.

To this objection the reply must be a *tu quoque*. The doctrine of the Trinity, which is at the very heart of Christian orthodoxy and taken in mainstream Christian traditions to be the test for admission to the Church by baptism, is nowhere in the Bible set forth as such. (The verse I John 5.7 is known to be a very late addition to the biblical text, not found in any of the ancient manuscripts.) Many of the doctrines that are accounted important in various central traditions of Christianity may be extrapolated from Scripture but are certainly not set forth there in the form in which they are presented in these traditions. The doctrine of the Trinity, in anything like the shape in which it is presented in the formulas used at Christian baptism, cannot be said to have been formulated earlier than the Council of Constantinople in A.D. 381. But then the New Testament itself did not take anything like its present shape until about the year 200 and some books, such as Hebrews, were disputed for long after that, while others, such as Barnabas and the Shepherd of Hermas, which are found in some of the great early manuscripts, were dropped. Even the contents of the Old Testament, as it is known to Protestants today, were not settled in Jewish tradition till about sixty years after the death of Christ. Moreover, this, the "Hebrew canon" of Scripture, does not include all the books of what the New Testament writers, for example, recognized as Scripture, since they used the Septuagint, a Greek version made about 250 B.C.E. for the Jews of the Diaspora. What, then, precisely, do we mean by "the Bible"?

Such questions are plainly far too complicated to be dealt with in any simplistic way such as demanding biblical proof texts. While Christianity needs a focus of testimony to the claims of Christian faith and this focus is rightly sought in Scripture, the Bible must be interpreted in one way or another and the principles of interpretation are, of course, open to question. To expect a mention of evolution or karma in the Bible is almost like expecting to find in it authority for the use of telephones or computers. Yet such concepts as evolution and karma can shed far more light on the meaning of the biblical message than any technological device could accomplish. We should therefore approach them with lively interest and curiosity, whether we account the Bible as of no particular importance or revere it as containing the very Word of God.

2

Evolution as Universal

> *A fire-mist and a planet,*
> *A crystal and a cell,*
> *A jelly-fish and a saurian,*
> *And the caves where the cavemen dwell;*
> *Then a sense of law and beauty,*
> *And a face turned from the clod—*
> *Some call it Evolution,*
> *And others call it God.*
>
> William Herbert Carruth,
> *Each in His Own Tongue*

When the concept of evolution is mentioned, most people's thoughts turn to Darwin's *The Origin of Species*. Naturally so, for Darwin's scientific work, controversial at the time, turned out to be epoch-making. His work was nevertheless also a catalyst for a much wider development that went far beyond the biological realm.

Let us look first, however, at the view to which Darwin's patient researches led him. Afterwards we shall consider his influence on later speculative thought about evolution as a universal principle of Being and consider also the antiquity of evolutionary theory.

Darwin, an indefatigable collector of facts, amassed an enormous amount of evidence to show that, historically, biological evolution has in fact taken place and that humanity is a product of it. The interpretation of this finding was and is plainly of crucial importance to those who believe in divine creation, since either evolution must be reconciled with such divine creation or else we must abandon the one or the other. The evidence Darwin amassed was overwhelming and has

11

thoroughly convinced the scientific community. Moreover, he showed that evolution *could* be accounted for in terms of purely "natural" causes. That is to say, there is no logical necessity for bringing in the notion of divine creation. Above all, he showed that the situation as we now know it cannot be accounted for by any hypothesis other than an evolutionary one. He and his contemporary A. R. Wallace simultaneously discovered the principle of natural selection, which very simply stated is the survival of the fittest in the struggle for existence. Precisely what is to be understood by "the fittest" demands interpretation; nevertheless, whoever they are, it is they who survive. Variation, heredity, and the struggle for existence combine in the evolutionary process. It is to their combination that he gave the term "natural selection." Let us look at these in turn before we go on.

First, variation: the fact that every individual is different from every other is extremely important. Of course dogs breed dogs and cats cats; yet within the same litter structural and functional differences can be observed. No less obviously, individual organisms are modified by environment. Differences in light and soil, for instance, affect plants, as every gardener knows. Still, whether the differences found in human beings and other higher animals can be entirely accounted for in such simple terms is, to say the least, questionable.

Second, heredity: there is no doubt that heredity plays an immense role in evolution. How mutations occur is not even now entirely clear. Geneticists dispute the nature of the process. But that they do occur and are observable is beyond dispute. Some organisms change very slowly over enormous ranges of time; others change quite rapidly. Genes, chromosomes, gametes, homozygotes and heterozygotes all play their parts. To specify with precision the cause of the mutations is, however, not by any means easy.

Third, struggle for existence: such is the vastness of the scale of reproduction alongside the fierce competition for space to live and the means of survival that only a small percentage of organisms do in fact survive. Bacilli and other microscopic organisms reproduce so rapidly and extensively that if one strain could somehow escape destruction by its competitors it would be able to take over its entire environment. Destruction is necessary to the evolutionary process, which is essentially a selective one. Again, the intensity of the struggle varies according to circumstance and place.

In view of a common misapprehension about the Darwinian theory of evolution, we ought to note carefully that Darwin expressly excluded the notion that natural selection necessarily implies a universal law of advancement or development. What it does, according to Darwin, is to take advantage of such variations that do arise and are beneficial to each creature under its complex relations of life. In other words, the evolutionary principle is one of adaptability. That species survives that is the most adaptable. Whether adaptability implies progress is another question. Certainly the strong do not necessarily survive; otherwise the dinosaur and the sabre-toothed tiger would surely have fared better than they did and man would have been extinct long ago. So the race is not always won by the strong. It would seem to be won, rather, by those skilled in adapting to circumstance; but then these would appear to be mentally strong in the sense of being skilled in the art, not so much of *savoir vivre* as of *savoir survivre.* These might be the cunning, the selfishly shrewd and by no means necessarily the most noble in character. If the meek do inherit the earth, then, according to Darwin, it must be because meekness is a clever strategy, not because it is typical of an "advanced soul." So then, if we are to go beyond Darwin's view we really do so under some banner other than the Darwinian one. Nevertheless, Darwin's theory may be *compatible* with some other interpretation of the nature of evolution.

We should also note that Darwin had immediate predecessors who in one way or another dealt with evolution along lines that might be said to have portended his own: Georges Louis Leclerc, Comte de Buffon (1707-1788), and Lamarck (1744-1829). Darwin's own grandfather Erasmus (1731-1802) also may be said to have foreshadowed (at least to some extent) his illustrious grandson.

The process of biological evolution is incalculably complex. Darwin himself perceived this and the work of later biologists has certainly not tended to reduce the complexity. Innumerable factors play their parts. Leaps seem to occur. moreover. in unpredictable ways. These critical turning points are no mere mutations. The move from atom to molecule, for instance, surely cannot be called mere mutation: the change is not so much a change of characteristics such as a change in a mammal from a round to an elongated head. It is more radical, more a movement to another dimension of Being. Then what of the leap from the inanimate to the animate, the emergence of life? Pass many millions of years and behold the even more startling and definitive leap to self-conscious mind. That is certainly no mere mutation such as a tendency to a squarer jowl or a hairier chest or a longer nose. To take a geometrical analogy. it does not compare to the difference between a square and a pentagon: it is. rather. like the difference between a square and a cube. a circle and a cylinder.

Darwin. Huxley. and their successors. each in his own way, saw all these problems. As naturalists, they followed approved, empirical, scientific methods. Argue as they might here and there about the precise form of the method for this or that purpose. they were at one in their general methodological direction. They very properly declined to go farther than their empirical methods would carry them—at least not in their working hours. They knew, however, that even the empirical methods used in biology must in some measure transcend those used in physics and chemistry. Then when we come to self-conscious mind even the empirical methods of biology must be modified. We can see rocks with our eyes and feel them with our fingers. We cannot so "see" life, but we can see living things and watch how they behave. We can also observe the behavior of thinking, self-conscious entities such as ourselves and can communicate with one another: yet by the methods of the biological sciences alone we cannot hope to understand the nature of the extremely complex ongoing process we call man, except in so far as he is describable as a mere biological entity. As medicine has advanced more in the last few decades than from the time of Aristotle to the nineteenth century, so the evolutionary process since the coming of man has entailed a far greater complexity than ever before on our planet. Before Darwin the antiquity of man was reckoned generally in terms of a few thousand years; since Darwin it has come to be seen in terms of millions. Even so, man is a comparatively recent development in relation to the age of our planet, which astronomers reckon at about 4½ billion years. Although some molecular formations may have begun four billion years ago, organisms more complex than algae probably did not appear till half a billion years ago. Forms of life such as man are so complex that they may be *comparatively* rare in the trillions of planets theoretically capable of developing such life forms.

Take at random some facts at the biological level that at least provide hints of the complexity of the genetic process in man. Because of chromosomal differences between males and females, males contribute more to the displayed characteristics (the phenotype) of the human race, while females contribute more to its stability. The twenty-third pair of chromosomes not only determines sex; it provides other genetic information. The male Y chromosome lacks some of the genetic material that the female possesses. So males exhibit some new traits and some new combinations of genes at a greater rate than do females. Recessive traits such as color blindness can occur in males when they possess only one gene to convey it; before a female can display this trait she must have two, the chance of which is so extremely small as to be negligible. A striking case is that of hemophilia B, which has plagued some of the royal families of Europe (e.g., Russian and Spanish), but only on the male side. If the mothers had "expressed" the trait in themselves rather than merely transmitted it, the disease would have killed them; but in fact they only transmitted it as a "carrier" transmits an infectious disease without contracting it himself. In some respects, then, nature seems to behave more experimentally with males. Females seem better equipped to preserve the stability of the human race, males to produce alterations in it. This does not, however, justify Spengler's sweeping assertion, "man makes history; woman is history," but, to a limited extent, it does perhaps lend some support to it.

Such known facts do indeed but hint at the genetic complexity of the human race. If human evolution be so complex at the biological level, what of the higher reaches of the human mind? What, too, of the future direction toward which the human race may be headed?

Biologists and anthropologists, from their patient observation and study, tell us much about how we have evolved, although some moves such as the "leaps" may remain mysterious. The future, however, is for obvious reasons unpredictable. The reason is simple. While we can guess at tendencies, as we can guess the general direction *likely* to be taken by a certain child, we can no more predict what future turns evolution will take than we can predict what the individual child will in fact turn out to be. From the parentage, disposition, gifts and shortcomings of individuals as they could have been known at, say, the age of five years, how could anyone have predicted how each would actually develop? For instance: Albert Schweitzer, Abraham Lincoln, Adolf Hitler, Mother Teresa, Greta Garbo? How, then, can we hope to predict with any confidence or in any detail what will be the outcome of the ongoing process we call *man*? The future of man is, to say the least, obscure. A predictive theory of biology is as impossible as is a predictive theory of history.

Nevertheless, if evolution occurs at all, it is in all probability a fundamental and universal principle. The great "process" thinkers of the past hundred years or so (e.g., Haeckel, Whitehead, Alexander, Wieman, Teilhard), much though they differ in their understanding of the relation between process and reality, all perceive, each in his own way, that fundamental and universal character of the evolutionary principle. The researches and discoveries of modern sciences lend strong support to *some form* of evolutionary ontology: the astrophysicists, for example, no less than the biologists. To put the matter in theological terms, we can no longer say only that evolution is God's way of doing certain things at certain stages of the creative process; it is, rather, the nature of the creative process at every stage. The galaxies exhibit this evolutionary character no less than do animal species on planet Earth. If, then it applies both to rocks and to living things, it surely applies no less to whatever mental and spiritual realities we recognize around us.

Although we cannot see the future of humankind in any detail, we can, by invoking our knowledge of the past, propose at least the strong probability that the future will not develop on lines *radically* different from the past. The process may be speeded up; it may take new and very unexpected turns; breakthroughs may occur introducing surprising novelties and plunging us into new and startling dimensions of existence; yet if the evolutionary process that we already know is the expression of a universal principle in Being, then the future surely cannot be *entirely* different from the past. Moreover, if we are to take seriously any religious prophecy or revelation about the future, we must interpret it in the light of the universal evolutionary principle.

We shall consider such speculative questions later in the development of our theme. For the present, let us glance at the history of notions about evolution before and after Darwin.

Evolutionary theories were by no means unknown in Greek antiquity. As early as the sixth century B.C.E., for example, the Greek thinker Anaximander, a pupil and younger contemporary of Thales, had proposed that all life, including human life, had come from the sea and had migrated to dry land. Anaximander thought, however, that man must have evolved from a special kind of species that had developed. He argued this from his observation that, while other creatures are self-supporting, man needs prolonged nursing, so that if he had had the same form as other creatures he could not have survived. So despite the marine origin of all biological entities, humanity is a special case. Plutarch (*c.* A.D. 46 - *c.* 120) reports that the Syrians actually revered fish as being, so to speak, our evolutionary ancestors. He attributes to Anaximander the view that human beings came into existence *within* fish. Then, having attained the capacity to look after themselves, they eventually came forth and took to the land.

Anaximander was, for his age, a remarkable thinker who held that there were many "worlds," all of them perishable, and all of them subject to the conflict of opposing forces, alternating between creation and destruction. They "suffer punishment" and they "make reparation to one another" for what he calls their respective "injustices." What he describes in this somewhat poetic way is the familiar Ancient Wisdom teaching of the karmic principle.

Aristotle (384-322 B.C.E.), one of the two greatest Greek philosophers whose writings have come down to us, could not be called an evolutionist in the modern sense; nevertheless his whole system involving potency and act, becoming and being, matter and form, provides the groundwork for an evolutionary view in which God, the Unmoved Mover, is the magnet that draws everything to himself. At least we may say that Aristotle, whose scientific interests were predominantly in the field of biology, was more disposed to an evolutionary outlook and system of thought than was his master Plato, whom he revered while in important respects departing from him.

The great Christian Church Father in the West, Augustine (A.D. 354-430), who was much influenced by Neoplatonic teachers, thought along very different lines. In looking at nature, however, he was impressed by the observation that the various species do not produce new species but go on producing the same: dogs produce dogs, roses roses, humans humans. Yet these species cannot properly be said to be the original cause of their respective offspring; otherwise presumably they would have had some choice in the matter; at least they would not have been so patently limited. Augustine developed the theory that God had implanted "seminal principles" (*rationes seminales*) into matter, setting into nature the potentiality for the emergence of the various species. The origin of species is to be found, then, in the creative mind of God. So Augustine held that Genesis must be, in effect, interpreted in order to be properly understood. God would not have created step by step, day by day, as a literalistic understanding of Genesis would suggest: he created all at once: that is, he simultaneously implanted into all species the seminal principles. Here again we have the makings of an evolutionary doctrine in Christian antiquity, although Augustine certainly did not actually develop one that would be readily identified as such today.

If we look at less philosophical and more exclusively religious writings in the West, we find that Christians were from the first constrained by their own beliefs and expectations to entertain some notion of an evolutionary pattern of history. For the first-century Christians generally held that the *parousia*, the end of the age, was at hand and that radical changes were about to take place. They had no systematic theory on the subject and their opinions were indubitably very diverse and extremely fluid: nevertheless, in one way or another they were all expecting changes and developments: a new age. Their recognition of changes that were taking place or about to take place suggests, to say the least, that change and development are not newcomers to the historic scene.

By the second century the expectation of a speedy end of the age was waning: yet the first-century mood left its imprint on later patristic thought. Montanus even calls a man who has been saved a *hyperanthrōpos*, a "superman," clearly envisioning no mere restoration through redemption by Christ but a new form of life for "bearers of the Spirit." It would be rash to read into such early passages an evolutionary theory comparable to those that became so fashionable in the late nineteenth century through the writings of Nietzsche and the plays of Ibsen and Shaw as well as the scientific studies of Darwin and other naturalists. Nevertheless, we can see that, even from the first, Christianity had within it the germs of evolutionary thought. In the early third century, Origen, the greatest Christian thinker and scholar in antiquity, provided a full-blown system that definitely implies evolutionism on a far grander scale than could have entered into the thinking of the average Christian in the Primitive Church.

Let us now turn our attention to more recent times. Darwin, toward the end of *The Origin of Species*, made some reflections on the moral implicates of his carefully developed scientific argument for his theory of biological evolution by natural selection. "When I view all beings not as special creations," he wrote, "but as the lineal descendants of some few beings which lived long before the first bed of the Silurian system was deposited, they seem to me to become ennobled." Nevertheless, to many who read him and T. H. Huxley, it seemed difficult to impute to the creative act of a beneficent deity a process that entailed the survival of the fittest by tooth and claw. Darwin claimed, however, to see grandeur in his view of life in which "from the war of nature, from famine and death, the most exalted object which we are capable of conceiving, namely the production of the higher animals, directly follows."[1]

Darwin recognized that in many cases only a very slight advantage on the part of a male could result in his success in competition with other males for the possession of a female and this biological superiority would generally result in his achieving a larger progeny. In this and in very many other ways, survival and evolution seemed to be the result of chance rather than of any creative design. The immediate effect of the book on the general public was to range them into two camps: those who were ready to accept such a view of the origin of man and those who vehemently rejected it as contrary to the Bible and who therefore insisted on an almost literal understanding of the biblical account of creation.

A generation or so later, however, some deeply religious thinkers in the Protestant tradition, thinkers still too little recognized, were arguing to the effect that the long, painful process of biological evolution is God's way of creating. Was it not more consonant with what the Bible teaches about the sacrificial love of God to suppose that if the universe, including man, is to be attributed to God's creative activity, God would work in this evolutionary way rather than by the creative wand-waving traditionally presented in popular Christian expositions? Did not such an evolutionary understanding of the creative process also better account for the

1. Charles Darwin, *The Origin of Species,* Chapter XIV. The original edition was published in 1859.

extraordinary organic complexity of man? Most of the writers I have in mind were American and long antedated the work of the Jesuit Pierre Teilhard de Chardin (1881-1955) who, out of the Catholic tradition, developed this theme along his own lines, bringing to bear upon it his scientific experience as a geophysicist. Ignorance of this genre of evolutionary Christian theology has led many to overrate Teilhard as a pioneer in the field. On the other hand, Teilhard, genius though he was, seems to have owed little if anything to these earlier thinkers, for he apparently shared the prejudices of his day that made it possible at that time for even some of the most enlightened European scholars to ignore American theology and American literature almost as if they did not exist.

Five men in particular should be noted as exponents of that pioneering work in the evolutionary interpretation of the Christian doctrine of creation. They were predominantly, though not entirely, Americans. Let us look at them briefly in turn:

1: John Fiske was born March 30, 1842, in Hartford, Connecticut, and was graduated from Harvard in 1863. An avid student of languages and literature, he remained for the rest of his life at Cambridge, Massachusetts, pursuing his work in philosophy and science. As a gifted writer, he contributed extensively to periodicals and was associated in various capacities with Harvard University. Proclaiming his ardent conviction that authentic religion and authentic science cannot be foes, he delivered, in 1871, a series of lectures on evolution. These, in a revised form, were eventually published in 1874 as *Outlines of Cosmic Philosophy*. His other works include *Darwinism*, 1879, and *Excursions of an Evolutionist*, 1883. Very influential on the thought of his day, he died July 4, 1901, at Gloucester, Massachusetts.

2. Lyman Abbott was born at Roxbury, Massachusetts, on December 18, 1835, was graduated from New York University in 1853 and admitted to the Bar in 1856. Having acquired an interest in theology, he was ordained a Congregationalist minister, held various pastorates, and turned increasingly to the editorship of journals that expressed his openminded

religious thought. In 1897 he published *The Theology of an Evolutionist.* Abbott taught that there are no laws of nature that are not laws of God's own being. God's way of doing things is the way of growth, development, evolution. "In so far as the theologian and the evolutionist differ in their interpretation of the history of life . . . I agree with the evolutionist." Yet he earnestly reaffirmed his unflinching belief in a "personal God."[2] He died in New York City October 22, 1922.

3. James McCosh was born of a Scottish Covenanting family in Ayrshire, April 1, 1811. Educated at Glasgow and Edinburgh, he was graduated M.A. from the latter university in 1834. After having been licensed by the Kirk as a preacher, he was among the many who participated in the Scottish Free Church movement ("the Disruption") in 1843. From 1851 till 1868 he taught logic at Queen's College, Belfast, being then invited to Princeton as Professor of Philosophy and President, positions that he held till his death on November 16, 1894. He received many honors, including a Harvard LL.D. Among his publications are *The Typical Forms and Special Ends in Creation,* published in 1855, and *The Religious Aspects of Evolution,* 1890.

4. Minot Judson Savage was born in Norridgewock, Maine, June 10, 1841. Because of poor health he could not attend college but eventually was graduated from Bangor Theological Seminary in 1864. After some years as a Congregationalist missionary in California and pastor in Massachusetts and elsewhere, he became a Unitarian, serving churches in Boston and Chicago and, from 1896 till his retirement in 1906, the Church of the Messiah, New York. Among his works are *The Religion of Evolution,* 1876; *Life Beyond Death,* 1901; *The Passing and the Permanent in Religion,* 1901; and *Men and Women,* 1902. He died May 22, 1918.

5. Henry Drummond (not to be confused with an older contemporary of the same name, the English politician who co-founded the Irvingite Church) was born in Stirling, Scotland, August 17, 1851, and educated at the University of

2. Lyman Abbott, *The Theology of an Evolutionist* (Boston: Houghton Mifflin Company, 1897), pp. 3-4, 9-10.

Edinburgh. He came under the influence of the American Moody-and-Sankey evangelical mission. In 1877 he became lecturer in "natural science" at the Free Church College, Glasgow, and in 1883 published his *Natural Law in the Spiritual World*. Having travelled in Africa and Australia, he gave the Lowell Lectures in Boston in 1893, published the following year as *The Ascent of Man*. In both of these works he expounded his evolutionary theology. He died March 11, 1897.

These men were not only of a religious temper; they came out of conservative Protestant backgrounds, remaining sympathetically attuned to their theologically conservative upbringing. Savage had preached missionary sermons during the California Gold Rush, but he came to perceive that Darwin's theory of evolution, so unpopular among conservative Protestants in his day, pointed to a divine Being greater than was encompassed in much traditional theology, and also to a more wonderful universe. He came to see Darwin as unwittingly having done a great service to religion. McCosh wrote in language that startlingly prefigures that of Teilhard, at a time when Teilhard was still a little boy. "The law of the spirit," he wrote, "is not an anomaly. It is one of a series; the last and the highest."[3] Drummond attached the evolutionary principle to the theological doctrine of election. "Quantity decreases as quality increases."[4] Even more dramatically anticipating Teilhard, he wrote: "Man . . . never knew till now . . . that his title deeds were the very laws of Nature, that he alone was the very Alpha and Omega of Creation, the beginning and the end of Matter, the final goal of Life."[5] Fiske summed up the whole of the new attitude by calling evolution simply "God's way of doing things," a phrase that Abbott and others echoed.

The notion that the slow, arduous process of evolution should be "God's way of doing things" is singularly persuasive

3. *The Religious Aspect of Evolution* (New York: Charles Scribner's Sons, 1890), p. 113.

4. *Natural Law in the Spiritual World* (New York: James Pott and Co., 1904), p. 389.

5. *The Ascent of Man* (New York: James Pott and Co., 1894), pp. 115-6.

to deeply religious minds who are open to the findings of modern science. The way in which the Darwinians presented the nature of the process, however, did sound like a challenge to religion as popularly understood. Darwinism seemed to assume that evolutionary advances, which sometimes came suddenly and after long periods of torpor, were the result of chance. At any rate, the Darwinians often seemed to make chance play a leading role in evolution. They recognized, of course, that intelligence and morality emerged in the process and that a point was reached in which the participants in the fierce struggle for existence came at last to see the advantage, indeed the necessity, of co-operation. This perception led to the development of social structures, of communities with laws and customs to protect the weak and educate the ignorant, or at least such of the latter as are capable of education. At least some men and women are filled with the highly ethical ideals and altruistic motives associated with the practice of the higher religions of humankind.

The process of attaining such higher reaches in the evolutionary ascent, however, still seems cruel and wild and amoral from where we stand. Rather we might expect a long, carefully planned educative scheme as the instrument of divine creativity. So from the available scientific evidence we are left with two reasonable choices. On the one hand, seeing order and purpose, we believe in a divine mind behind the evolutionary process; on the other hand, seeing none, we attribute it all to chance. Both of these views can be persuasively argued. Neither can be conclusively proved. All depends on an individual's perception of cosmic purpose.

Sir Fred Hoyle and other distinguished astronomers have more recently proposed a startling and challenging theory. Noting that human beings depend for their functioning on 200,000 chains of amino acids, arranged in a particular pattern, Fred Hoyle began a lecture at the Royal Institution, London, by pointing out that the odds against arriving at such a pattern by accidental process were comparable to those against throwing five million consecutive sixes at dice. Although not purporting to provide a "religious" explanation for the existence of intelligent life on our planet Earth, he felt that it must have been planned or designed in some way under intelligent direction. The amazing order found in the bio-materials are such that they must be the result of intelligent design. Having been for many years among those who have researched the possibility of influences from outer space, he has expounded the view that the Earth may have been bombarded with microorganisms from extraterrestrial sources, causing such diseases as influenza and virus colds. The gaps that the Darwinians recognized in the evolutionary process point, he contends, to periods of very rapid change, which may have been provoked by viruses and other influences carried by such microorganisms in such a way as to cause a jolt within the evolutionary process and so lead to a change in its direction. Whatever the merit of such a theory, which need not particularly concern us here, its proponents do call to our attention the extraordinarily mysterious character of the evolutionary process, in which natural selection explains so much yet also leaves so much unexplained.

The fortuitous concurrence of events provides the most far-fetched explanation of the process by which humanity eventually emerged and produced a Plato and a Kant, a Leonardo and a Shakespeare. While natural forces such as bring about the growth of trees, the occurrence of earthquakes, and the flow of rivers have played their part in the process, something more is needed to account for the enigma of intelligent life. That the will-to-live assumes in its earlier forms the crude violence we see in primitive forms of life is understandable; nor is it difficult to see how eventually it might give place to subtler motives and more highly organized structures and modes of conduct. Yet in the mystery of man is so much that demands fuller explanation. The more we appreciate the achievements and the capacities of man as well as his limitations, the more we must surely be forced to recognize that behind, or in, or with the creative process is at work a higher intelligence of some sort. To say roundly that "God created humanity" and other forms of life is a very abbreviated, shorthand way of describing the process; nevertheless, it is surely less misleading than is the attribution of all to chance. That the emergence of values such as human intelligence and human awareness of duty may be expected to take billions of years is now clear enough; no less clear must it be that they cannot have been entirely self-generated but must have required the guidance of intelligence higher than ourselves. Yes, and much more than intelligence as we know it.

The "law" of karma, familiar to all students of Indian thought, is the moral and spiritual balance in all things that keeps this evolutionary process on (as we might say) an even keel. It is our way of expressing the nature of the omnipresent action of divine Being. It may be called, if we prefer such language, the moral side of God, entailing his righteousness, his mercy, and above all his love. Though this idea occurs in many religions, Christians see all of these displayed most perfectly in the action of God in his complete self-revelation in Christ. What is there revealed to Christians is *not* that God, in an extreme emergency, can show himself to be able to rescue humanity from a mess into which it has fallen; what is revealed is that in the Incarnation of God in Christ the nature of God's action throughout the creative process is shown with particular clarity. The Incarnation is a dramatic way of showing what the creative process entails: the outpouring of an everlastingly sacrificial love into that process, in the course of which has emerged man, the slice of that line of the process that is where we now are.[6]

In times past, when physicists could still talk of the workings of the universe in mechanistic terms, it was natural, if not inevitable, that many should think of karma in a comparable way as a sort of cosmic moral bookkeeping. While such a view of karma is not an entirely false one, it is, to say the least, something of a caricature. Karmic forces are always present, but it is precisely where the mechanistic aspect of things gives place to individuality, selfhood, freedom of choice, and personality, that they begin to show themselves in new

6. I have discussed this in my *He Who Lets Us Be* (New York: Seabury Press, 1975).

and striking ways. Where, in the earlier stages of the evolutionary process, the individual has been in large measure a prisoner of these karmic forces, he now begins to work *with* them and in so doing consciously to shape his or her own karma. As I develop my self-awareness, catching myself in the very act of my becoming, I begin to take charge of my own destiny, not by any means through defiance of karma but through cooperation with it. I learn "to live with myself" neither by passive acquiescence in what is handed to me on a platter nor by anger at my lot. I come to peace through understanding that my circumstances are given me for a reason (usually a very complex one) and that whatever be that reason my function in the process is to surmount (not circumvent) the obstacles in my path. I must work my way through my circumstances according to the karmic rules. I may even make rules for myself as I mature in the process of spiritual evolution. But I must never spiritually "jump ship" or become morally A.W.O.L., for doing so is futile. To try to cheat karma is to cheat myself. Nevertheless, I can, so to speak, woo the karmic forces by obedience to them and so win them on to my side in the evolutionary process.

Liberation is what spiritual evolution is all about. To be liberated is to evolve. It is, however, a commonplace of religious experience that moral and spiritual liberation is not easily attained; nor is it ever what it seems at first sight to be. All the religions teach us, each in its own way, to ask for strength to carry our burdens, to walk a hard road, to climb a steep mountain: never to ask to be relieved of a burden, to find an easy bypass, to discover a chairlift up that mountain. Suicide is at once the most obvious liberation from life with all its immediate problems and the most tragically constricting and spiritually damaging response to the gift of life. For in suicide the person builds up against himself or herself a tremendous wall of karma that must be surmounted in another life or other lives. It puts back the karmic clock.

Genuine liberation is attained only by coming to terms with the karmic principles that express the very nature of divine Being. In Christian terms, we are liberated from sin, which is what alienates us from God and hinders our spiritual progress. Sin is at once blindness to and defiance against the holiness of divine Being: resistance to the love that is at the heart of the graciousness of that Being. Sin is no mere disobeying of an item in a code of laws, nor is it even aptly described as a failure to do one's known duty: it is, rather, an unwillingness to accept growth. To obstruct divine love, to stop its flow in our inmost being, is to stunt our spiritual growth at its very roots: to infuse it into our life is to insure evolutionary progress.

There is no one way of doing this. Methodologies have their role in spiritual evolution as in all other enterprises: yet in climbing a mountain it matters less that you follow this instructor or that, use this kind of boot or that, than that you reach the summit. The karmic law is the principle that insures the fulfillment of our destiny irrespective of the paths we choose to attain it. Samuel Johnson expressed in the opening lines of his much-loved hymn the notion that karmic principle is wider than any formulation of it:

City of God, how broad and far
Out spread thy walls sublime!
The true thy chartered freemen are
Of every age and clime.

One may become bogged down, however, in what Henri Bergson called a static morality and stultified in what he called a closed type of religion. Doing so is somewhat like getting into a habit of diet or dress or study or posture that is not in itself bad but tends to exclude development and change. The creative, dynamic force is stifled, impeding evolutionary advance. The person can then become more and more a slave to his own limiting karma instead of using his inbuilt creative instinct to transcend such karmic enslavement and discover the freedom that is within himself. That is where help is needed, not for anyone to do one's work for one, for not even God can do that, but to lift or jolt one out of the morass. This need not be a morass of sin but merely a stultifying habit, for as the French saying has it: the best is the enemy of the good.

Such is the karmic law that in spiritual growth we dare never for long stand still.

We may also be unwittingly hindered by acceptance of a conventional metaphysical stance. For example. Christian thought has been. despite its strongly theocentric emphases. remarkably anthropocentric in its understanding of the creative purposes of God. One wonders. indeed. in reading Genesis. how the angels. good ones or bad. ever got there in the first place! Traditionally. the Judaeo-Christian view of creation seems to presuppose that God created everything for the sake of man. the supreme triumph of his creative skill. In Islam this tendency is even more marked. Yet surely what commands our interest in man. apart from the parochial concern arising from the fact that we happen to belong to the human process. is that in man we can discern something of the way in which at least one current of the evolutionary process is going. F. R. Tennant (1866-1957) was among those who. in writing on the philosophical foundations of Christian theology. perceived more clearly than many in his generation that the "progressiveness" of the evolutionary process as seen in humanity suggests that it is directed to an end beyond humanity. Man is unlikely. to say the least. to be the final stage in the evolutionary process or the highest finite being in the cosmos. the culmination of the work of the creative power of God. On the contrary. he saw that there may be other rational beings in other realms. beings far ahead of us. He also saw that the creatures we call the "lower creation" on this planet are not necessarily "mere by-products of the making of humanity" with no purpose of their own in the scheme of things.[7] More must be said on that in a later chapter in which we are to consider our kinship with other forms of life.

A similarly evolutionary theme is still more strikingly developed in the work of Bergson who put evolution at the center of his thinking. Born in 1859. the year of the publication of Darwin's celebrated work. Bergson wrote several books leading up to his *L'Evolution créatrice*. which appeared in 1907.

7. F. R. Tennant. *Philosophical Theology* (Cambridge: Cambridge University Press. 1928-30). Vol. II. pp. 113-14.

He described evolution as a vital impulse (*élan vital*), which drives all organisms toward more and more complex and higher modes of organization. Its creative power runs through all things and is the fundamental reality in all things. Intellect, important though it be, is only derivative. By intuition we can discover the nature of reality in a way that is opaque to the intellect because the intellect by its very nature turns the dynamic into the static.

Bergson thought that the Darwinians had not been able to give adequate accounts of the way evolution works precisely because they had not recognized the *élan vital* in all organisms. For instance, Darwin had referred to variations but he had not really explained their cause. Hugo De Vries had pointed to the mutations that led certain members of a species to develop variations conducive to their survival, but he too failed to explain how this occurred. Darwinians wrote as though a change somehow occurred in some part of the organism, slowly or suddenly; they did not appreciate the principle of the *élan vital* that protected, so to speak, the functional unity of an organism. So they could not explain how successive changes could occur in an organism without injuring continuity of function. Lamarck had attributed changes to a special effort the organisms made, but he could not explain how such changes could be passed on to future generations of the species. Bergson approved of Lamarck's "effort" hypothesis but accounted it inadequate without a principle such as that of the *élan vital* to support it.

The *élan vital*, according to Bergson, must in some way resemble what we call consciousness, which is to say that consciousness is present even in the most rudimentary forms of life. From this *élan vital* emerges life itself with all its manifold possibilities. So fundamental is the *élan vital* that Bergson is willing to call it "of God, if not God himself." The notion that God evolves with evolution is found in thinkers such as the British Samuel Alexander and the American Henry Nelson Wieman. Bergson, however, did not follow that line, seeing God, rather, as the fundamental principle *behind* the evolutionary process. His thought on the subject leaves full scope for freedom of choice, for although the *élan vital* is ever at work within the process, the final goal, the *telos*, cannot be predetermined. Authentic novelty may be found at every step of the way. Moreover, the intuition with which consciousness is endowed is the most dependable guide we have, since it apprehends the flow of life, not a static picture of it. Of course it is often useful and may indeed be necessary to stop the motion picture and examine a still; but the still can never be a substitute for the motion picture.

Applying this general principle to religion. Bergson points out that religion may be either static or dynamic. Religion is a fundamental element in human consciousness and as such it is not at all obstructive to genuine intellectual inquiry. When, however, it becomes static, having crystallized into institutional forms, it tends to take on an anti-intellectual outlook to protect itself from development and change. So conventional religion. Bergson says, is a derivative perversion of a once-living reality. Dynamic religion is mystical rather than institutional and therefore individual rather than social. So such dynamic religion achieves much more directly the vision of God that is the aim of all authentic religion. Static, conventional religion, when it achieves this at all, does so under great difficulties, in face of many grave obstacles, and in the end opaquely at best.

Bergson and those of his contemporaries such as Alfred North Whitehead, who sought in other ways to show the organic unity of all things, were reacting against a widespread tendency to take sets of facts in isolation from other sets of facts. They contended that no coherent philosophy can be built by such means. More importantly, such a tendency causes our inbuilt capacity for intuiting reality to be obscured if not destroyed.

What we have seen of the development of evolutionist ideas since Darwin published *The Origin of Species* shows us abundantly that evolution, no less than any other theory leading to a perception of or insight into reality, may be interpreted spiritually or otherwise. The universe around us does not *compel* us to recognize a divine principle within it, in the sense that anyone who fails to recognize it must be accounted mentally deficient as would be, for instance, a person who failed to recognize that the angles of a triangle must equal two right angles. One may be both sane and in possession of an excellent computer-like brain, yet lack the spiritual sensitivity that enables one "to see God." If, however, one does see beyond the process to the principle behind it, one must certainly ask how the principle that governs the evolutionary process operates at moral and spiritual levels. Biologists tell us something of how it operates in lower forms of life, for instance among caterpillars and ants; but if evolution is an ongoing process among humans, how does it work at levels in which moral and spiritual qualities and concerns become more highly developed? Is there an identifiable way in which the principle is worked out at such reaches of the human consciousness and at such stages in the evolutionary pilgrimage?

Of course there is. It is called, perhaps somewhat loosely, the karmic principle. This principle or "law" is expressed under different guises in the various religions of the world; but it is certainly no stranger to any of them, by whatever name it may be called. We reap what we sow. None of the great religions of the world denies this; each in one way or another explicitly affirms it. In the spiritual realm as in the physical, every event has a cause and every cause has its effect. At first sight such a "law" sounds too rigid, too inexorable, to fit a principle of development and growth such as evolution must be. Before we go further, therefore, we should look carefully at the nature of the karmic principle so as to examine how it may function in the evolutionary process.

3

The Moral Dimension of Evolution

Stern Lawgiver! yet thou dost wear
The Godhead's most benignant grace;
Nor know we anything so fair
As is the smile upon thy face:
Flowers laugh before thee on their beds
And fragrance in thy footing treads;
Thou dost preserve the stars from wrong;
And the most ancient heavens, through thee,
are fresh and strong.
　　　　　William Wordsworth, *Ode to Duty*

Karma is a Sanskrit word. Literally it means *action*. As with many words in the vocabulary of the religions of the world, it has acquired a special ethical connotation. It means the principle governing cause and effect in the spiritual realm. In Buddhism it connotes the principle according to which an action performed for personal gratification results in a moral effect. *Karma* is closely associated in Indian thought with the concept of *dharma*, which (somewhat like *li* in Chinese thought) is such a basic spiritual concept that it may be translated in many ways; for example, as duty, mercy, righteousness. *Karma*, like *dharma*, is one of those words expressing an idea with roots so deeply embedded in language and stretching so far back into the mists of pre-history and oral culture that our difficulty in understanding them springs not from their complexity but from ours. They are too simple, too basic, for us to grasp with our complex mentality and our highly developed capacity for making subtle distinctions. Another example is the Greek word *dikē*, which means literally *way* or *path*, but has come to mean *the right* or *the ethical*; that is,

33

the right way, the way of righteousness.

The karmic principle, then, is the moral law of cause and effect that runs through all spiritual as well as all other aspects of existence. To think of it as a fatalistic principle is radically to misunderstand it, for it is nothing if not a freewill principle. Even to think of it as a system of punishment and reward is a distortion, for that is only one aspect of karma, a view from a particular stance. Karma operates in the spiritual realm as surely as does the "law" of gravity in the physical world, and as we can be taught to use gravity to our physical advantage, so we can learn to make the karmic principle work for our spiritual growth.

To do so, however, we must have at least some vision of evolutionary purpose. We cannot expect to hold to the right course, let alone to rise to higher dimensions of existence, if we do not even know the lie of the land. As one theosophical writer puts it, "till a man understands the plan of evolution, there is no great change in him from life to life; there are the usual ups and downs of good and evil fortune, of griefs and joys, as years pass and lives are lived." He goes on to say that it is only when a man understands the evolutionary plan and lives "not for himself but for his fellow-men, that great changes take place in his karma, and his evolution is hastened. Then his progress is swift from life to life, even as in the ratio of geometrical progression."[1] The same writer even begins his book by defining theosophy as "the wisdom arising from the study of the evolution of life and form."[2] So close is the connection between evolution and the karmic principle that is at the heart of the Ancient Wisdom.

But how can the karmic principle, essentially one of moral and spiritual balance and harmony, fit on the one hand a naturalistic doctrine of evolution and, on the other, the notion of divine initiative that is found in many of the great religions, for instance, the Christian doctrine of grace? If we are to understand evolution in its spiritual dimension and relate it

1. C. Jinarajadasa, *First Principles of Theosophy* (Adyar, Madras: The Theosophical Publishing House, 1960), p. 108.
2. Ibid, p. 1.

to the moral and spiritual "laws" that govern all action, we must have an appropriately large map. And if we are to take seriously the testimony of the seers and mystics of the great religions of the world, we must be able to see how the "grace" they talk about can function in that map of the evolutionary process, restoring rather than upsetting the spiritual balance apart from which the map must be unintelligible. To the concept of grace a special chapter will be devoted.

First let us consider how karma can fit a Darwinian type of theory. The earlier followers of Darwin sometimes did interpret biological evolution as a merely tooth-and-claw affair in which brute strength prevailed; but of course, were that the case, man would not have survived, since he does not even begin to compare with elephants and lions and tigers in physical might. Ingenuity, adaptability, and organizational powers obviously play a crucial role in survival. As we rise in the evolutionary scale, however, other factors appear. As the individual learns that he cannot hope to survive alone, he joins with others to obtain protection for himself and, as a *quid pro quo*, to provide it for others.

All this may be seen already at work in the animal kingdom. In us humans, however, it is developed in special ways. Setting aside ethical questions about the nature of what we call altruism (whether it is merely disguised egoism, for instance), we do recognize that in human relationships a new element emerges, at least among highly developed human beings: an element expressed in the notion of disinterested, sacrificial love. The power of such love in protecting and developing the character of individuals within the group and so promoting their survival is certainly impressive. For while a mere social-contract kind of morality can fall apart as soon as the contract no longer seems to be working well, genuine love is by no means so easily destroyed. From it flows an immense sense of responsibility for the welfare of others, if only (at first) for others in the group in which the love prevails. It is no longer a business type of arrangement, no longer a mere mutual back-scratching agreement. As a devoted parent will give a kidney to save a child's life, so one individual in a group will sacrifice even life itself for the good of the community to which he belongs and to which he feels he owes more than he can ever repay.

The karmic principle expresses the fundamental moral principle in a basic form: "we reap what we sow." To live by the sword is to perish by the sword. By an inexorable moral and spiritual law, everything I do has consequences: my good acts have good consequences for me; my bad acts bad consequences. These consequences may follow quickly; they may take a long time; indeed, according to the reincarnational view that is traditionally associated with karma, they may take several lives to be worked out in full. Yet the karmic principle is much more than a merely mechanical, computerized kind of moral bookkeeping. It encompasses, as we shall presently see, the working out of the law of love itself. For love, too, has its laws and we shall see that they operate according to the basic evolutionary principle of Being, although only to those at a comparatively advanced level of consciousness are they discernible. Although some of us may claim, in the manner of Leibniz, to see the rudiments of freedom and of higher motivations even at primitive levels of development, these unfold in their splendor only at the higher levels.

Recognition of the karmic principle brings pure joy to the minds of those who have grasped it. Of none is this more true than of Christians who have adopted the idea and put it at the center of their thought. For it symbolizes all that is at the heart of Christian faith as seen and as lived in the light of an eternal principle of spiritual evolution. Most educated Christians nowadays accept the principle of evolution in biology. Nevertheless, many still think (though they may know better) in old-fashioned, pre-evolutionary terms, much as many intelligent people, despite what they know of quantum physics and relativity theory, persist in outmoded Newtonian modes of thought about the universe.

True, the law of karma might so be interpreted as to express what old-fashioned Christian theologians called the wrath of God, the eternal justice at the core of divine Being; but it expresses no less his eternal mercy. Above all it expresses God's infinitely sacrificial love. It wholly eliminates the crude anthropomorphic concepts of God as sitting like a judge in a law court on the Day of Judgment. Nor does the karmic principle present us with a vision of our passing or flunking a cosmic examination after an indeterminate yet always brief amount of time allotted and with no chance of a second attempt before the final reckoning of our destiny: heaven or hell forever. On the contrary, karma, inexorable though it be, affords us unlimited opportunities to improve our conduct and our adjustment to the nature of divine Being. Its workings reflect the character of the God who stands behind the injunction of Jesus to forgive our brother not seven times but "seventy times seven" (Matthew 18.22).

Karma exhibits the eternal compassion of God, who not only gives us unlimited time to work out our salvation but efficaciously leads us to the most direct path to higher consciousness and eternal life. The Bible generally tends to express these truths in the picturesque imagery of a paternal promise, but they are more: they are a divine principle written into the very Being of God. To know the law of karma is to be constantly hearing the authentic music of God himself. It is to know that all is indeed well, since God is continually purifying us as one purifies gold and silver in the furnace (Malachi 3.3). So although our human life is often more struggle than hymn, we are always hearing the voice of angels above the noise of battle. The karmic principle is our surety of the permanence of God's Being and the thoroughness of all his works. When Christian theologians talk as they do of God's Word and its dependability, it is this principle that they attest. It is a principle at the core of all deeply religious thought.

To live in such constant awareness is therefore not only to live according to an eternal principle of duty, although it does entail this; it is at the same time to enjoy that serene confidence that Jesus exhibited in all his words and deeds. Great souls have all understood, each in his or her own way, the reality of karma, even though they may never have heard the word. (We remember how Molière's Monsieur Jourdain was pleased to know that he had been talking prose all his

life. although nobody had ever told him.) Whenever you find
anyone living in complete confidence in God you may be sure
that that person has grasped the fundamental principle of
karma. even though it be without ever having heard of it. To
the question of the nature of this assurance a special chapter
will be devoted later.

In karma we see that nothing is overlooked. Not a sparrow
falls to the ground without God's knowledge (Matthew 10.29).
Nothing is wasted: nothing is lost. Justice may take long to
work out. but it shall prevail. As Longfellow paraphrases an
old Greek proverb. "Though the mills of God grind slowly,
yet they grind exceedingly small." We can cheat ourselves for
a time. but we cannot cheat God. Others may mock us even as
they treat us with cruelty and deal us flagrant injustices. acting
as if there were no reckoning: but. to the extent of our attunement to the karmic principle. we know that the moral law
pervades everything and that those who wrong us are building
up for themselves grievous obstacles to their own spiritual
evolution. They are making prisons for themselves. God does
not send them to prison or otherwise administer punishment
to them: they do it to themselves. Under the karmic principle
they are haunted by their evil deeds in such a way that they
build the walls of their own prison and manufacture the whip
of their own flagellation.

So it is not for us to wreak vengeance upon them. In one
way or another they must and they will work out the consequences of their deeds. however long the process may take.
Knowing this. the consequence of our own thoughtless words
and evil deeds is awesomely clear. We are gloriously free to do
whatever we can and will: but our awareness of the karmic
principle sets before our eyes a vision of the results of irresponsible action. Karma attunes us to moral responsibility.
Our only fear comes from what we are doing to ourselves. All
this accords in every way with the spirit of the noblest and
most characteristic teaching of the Bible and the Christian
classics as well as of the Scriptures of the other religions
of the world.

One of the great consolations that attend recognition of the karmic principle and make it so attractive to so many lies in its explanatory function. It explains life at a deeper level than any to which we are accustomed in ordinary reflection about life. It explains, for instance, why our lives seem at once both orderly and chaotic, both purposeful and purpose-less, why we see glimmers of purpose yet cannot by any means see purpose at every point The reason is that we are looking at only a brief chapter in a very long story. That our lives are brief, whether they are a hundred years or only a few days, is a truth that sages from time immemorial have noted. A very long and full life can sometimes help people to catch a glimpse of what lies beyond this present life, but many live long lives without ever seeing more than they could have learned in childhood. Only by understanding something of the law of karma and the rebirths it entails can we begin to appreciate that even the longest of lives is but a slim chapter in an inconceivably long story. Living a single life cannot by itself give us an adequate perspective on the basic question that all great thinkers have asked in one way or another: "Why am I here?" Fascinating as I may find the panorama of my present life, the more deeply my consciousness of it is developed the more I must see it as only a few moments of the unimaginably long film that is my history. That rebirth is an implicate of the karmic principle will be discussed later.

What then, is this life span in face of the vast multidimen-sional cinematography that is the story of the universe? Yet that little run of film that is my own present life is unique and infinitely precious to me, since it is I who am making it. God, who is ever "letting me be," graciously permits me to be master of my destiny. As we have already seen, karma is nothing if not a freewill principle. My freedom is bounded, of course, by the circumstances that are thrown at me because of my past actions (as Sartre puts it, *je te là, comme ça*); neverthe-less, within these limits my freedom is infinite.

The essence of my life consists indeed in a vast number of personal decisions that my freedom makes possible, within a variety of circumstances that circumscribe my acts. These decisions are bound up with my spiritual evolution. The most significant of them in terms of that evolution are not those that I make in following a safe, much-trodden path, laid out according to the precepts of a traditional moral code (useful as this may be in my general spiritual development) but, rather, when I am in an unexplored wilderness lacking a moral map to guide me. My guide is my conscience, whose reliability depends on how well I am informed and, in the last resort, on my own spiritual maturity. The precepts taught in every religion in no way relieve me of decisions at every turn. For example, Jesus' injunction "So always treat others as you would like them to treat you; that is the meaning of the Law and the Prophets" (Matthew 7.12, Jerusalem Bible) is a formulation of the eternal moral law that is to be found in all the major religions of the world; yet I must discover for myself exactly how I am to act in a given situation. The precept itself raises a variety of subtle distinctions. For instance, if I were guilty of, say, drunk driving, I should not like to be put in jail and to be deprived of my drivers license for a long period of time; yet that is what I and many other concerned citizens have for long urged. In so urging, however, am not I doing to someone else precisely what I should not like to have done to myself?

Again, I might feel that if I were a waiter I should like to be treated in a certain way, but this waiter that is serving my table is apparently not at all of my opinion. By treating him with friendliness I may think to obey the Golden Rule, since that is what I believe I should like were I in his shoes. I am not, however, not in his shoes, and I find in fact that he wishes to be treated with aloofness, at least so long as we are in the relationship in which we stand while he is waiting on me. The Golden Rule seems to assume that everyone knows how everyone else would like to be treated and that, moreover, I know how I should like to be treated if I were somebody else. That appears to be not at all the case. I do not really know enough about you to tell whether you would relish my treating you the way I think I should like you to treat me if our positions were reversed. I cannot follow the Golden Rule without making judgments.

The word *conscience* means simply consciousness. According to the karmic principle, the moral consciousness of each individual varies enormously, depending on the training and discipline that has helped to develop it over a long succession of lives. It is the outcome of a very long history. Even dogs and cats have in-built instincts that protect them; so we, at a more advanced level, have learned that certain courses of action are to be avoided because of the ill effects they bring in their train, while others are to be pursued because of the beneficial results that attend them. The individual conscience is not reliable *per se*, since its reliability depends on its development through that long history. Hence, the immense variation in sensitivity. That is why we sometimes are wise to be guided by others (a master, guru, or director) farther advanced in spiritual development. Our greatest progress, however, is made when we make good decisions on our own; leaps of faith, as Kierkegaard has called them. Making such decisions always entails risk. They may turn out to be wrong, as do many a scientist's experimental hypotheses. That is why following rules is the safer course. In great moral crises, however, the individual has to make his or her own rules, and it is here that a mature and strongly developed conscience is of priceless value. Such uncharted areas also offer the opportunity for learning and growth.

All this shows that kinship of karmic doctrine with modern existentialism. The basic questions that existentialists raise are the ones to which the karmic principle provides the answers. Questions such as "Who am I?" and "Why am I here?" and "Where am I going?" are all questions that already *presuppose* an outlook governed in some way or other by a recognition, however dim, of a rational principle in the universe, such as the karmic one. Those modern philosophers who object to such questions, accounting them unintelligible or pseudo-questions, do so partly because they resist the recognition of the karmic principle. Yet these are the very questions that people who have no such artificial intellectual axe to grind find the most obvious as well as the most profound, reflecting the deepest human concerns.[3] To understand the nature of the universe and learn of the behavior of the galaxies and of the geophysical structure of our own planet ought indeed to be of interest to every intelligent human being; nevertheless, when my experience teaches me the uniquely incalculable value of the moral pilgrimage in which I find myself engaged, existentialist types of questions are infinitely more pressing. The karmic principle is the key to answering them.

In the history of philosophy, existentialism is commonly set in opposition to the thought of the great rationalists such as Leibniz and Spinoza, because it calls attention to the reality of freedom of choice and to an "irrational" element for which the traditional "rationalisms" seem to provide no adequate place. The karmic law, however, is by no means a philosophical "hard determinism" in which every event is predetermined by principles that leave no room for freedom of choice. As we have already seen abundantly, it is anything other than that.

A succinct definition of determinism is impracticable. Not only does it take several forms (e.g., ethical, psychological, ontological); it comes in varying degrees of strictness. Characteristic of a *thoroughgoing* determinism, however, would be the view that no event could ever be other than it is. It is not merely that every event has a cause or causes; there is no "room" for any agent to act freely or independently at all, so that the concept of freedom of choice or action is meaningless. Some degree of determinism is inevitable; we ought, therefore, not to decide *for* or *against* determinism, but to ask *how much* freedom is one to acknowledge within a determined structure. Recognition of the karmic principle entails the acknowledgement of the possibility of whatever freedom is needed for the agent's evolution and growth. Any degree at all of moral freedom precludes a thoroughgoing determinism.

It is the rationality of the karmic principle that has made it

3. For the connection between the preoccupations of modern existentialism and the basic outlook of the Ancient Wisdom, see my *Gnosis* (Theosophical Publishing House, 1979), Chapter IV.

so attractive to the most diligent seekers after the truth about our human destiny. For although rationality is not the key to an understanding of all things, no progress can be made in understanding anything where reason is flouted or abused. Thinkers from the earliest times have rightly sought for causes. Although we have come to see in the history of thought that causation is far more complex than was formerly supposed, the basic concept of causation is not on that account to be abandoned. Many have sought causes in physical and chemical processes and have tried to explain all conditions and all events in terms of them. Of course physical and chemical processes do provide explanations; but we must face the important philosophical problem of what constitutes explanation. Let us look at this question.

If you ask me to explain why the street is wet, I may very well "explain" the phenomenon by telling you that it had been raining. That may be a perfectly adequate explanation in the circumstances and for the purpose in hand. You did not know that it had been raining. You thought, perhaps, that neighbors had been overwatering their front yards. I provide you with an "explanation" that satisfies you quite well. If, however, you were to be more persistent, you might go on to demand why it rained. I might perhaps try to stem the flow of your intellectual curiosity by telling you that there were very black clouds that have now passed over. You, in turn, would probably object that you had often seen black clouds that precipitated no rain at all. Seeing your intractability, I might then call in a professional meteorologist to give a more scientific explanation than my meager meteorological knowledge could provide. What philosophers from Hume onwards have seen, however, is that the "causes" in terms of which the sciences provide "explanations" are not "necessary" causes; that is, we do not really observe them or know them as belonging to the essential nature of things; we merely notice that certain events always follow certain conditions and are not found apart from these conditions, and so we call the relationship one of cause and effect. We do so rightly, for there we have the best "explanation" we can expect to find from sciences such as physics and chemistry, and so the professional meteorologist's explanation, for example, is infinitely better than my mere observation that rain had fallen, "causing" the wetness of the street. To recognize the reality of moral causes, however, is to see that we can never *exhaust* the explanatory process by giving only physical and chemical explanations, invaluable though these be for many important purposes in life.

We cannot hope to know the moral causes of everything. Scientists do not know even the physical and chemical causes of the phenomena that demand "explanation." Physicians habitually deal in causes and effects. Why you broke your leg is easily explained in terms of physics: a horse kicked it or you fell downstairs. A precise, detailed account of the cause of the fracture could very well be provided. Even a chronic condition such as pernicious anaemia might be genetically accounted for or otherwise sufficiently well "explained" to satisfy a group of well-trained pathologists and physiologists. An unfortunate genetic inheritance might indeed be a good explanation so far as it went and certainly a great deal better than an attribution to bad luck or ill fate. Yet it might well be not the whole explanation; no more, indeed, than was my "it was raining" a total explanation for the wetness of the street. What if, for instance, the sufferer had caused so much bloodshed in a previous life that, as Gina Cerminara has suggested in such a case, his own body had become "the field of slaughter," symbolically "the sacrificial altar on which his crime was expiated," exhibiting a "protracted form of educative justice"?[4]

Far-fetched as this may sound to many, let those who find it so reflect on the astounding powers of the mind to bring about physical illness in the present life. Every experienced physician knows at least something of the astonishing extent to which physical ills may be brought on by mental conditions. Can anyone doubt, for instance, the evil effects upon the human body of habitual hatred or insatiable avarice or

4. Gina Cerminara, *Many Mansions* (New York: William Sloane, 1950), pp. 53-4.

paroxysms of anger or gnawing resentment or self-centered, narcissistic preoccupations? Of course our mental attitudes and habits immensely affect the welfare of our bodies. Yet if we accept the general principle behind these now almost commonplace observations, what are we to say of congenital endowments such as an exceptionally healthy body or congenital defects that lead to grievous physical and mental impairment? These cannot be attributed to anything we have thought or said or done, anything we have mentally caused in this life. The karmic principle, however, with its reincarnational implicates, provides a better, that is, a fuller explanation than is available from genetics alone.

What I am suggesting here is implicit in the teaching of the Bible, not least the New Testament. It runs through all the Christian classics. To be sure, they use their own traditional symbols and special language to express such ideas in their own way, often with a directness and childlike simplicity that is very beautiful and drives home the basic ideas to the minds of men and women in memorable and picturesque ways. Christianity inherited its most characteristic modes of symbolization from its Semitic ancestor, the religion of the Hebrew people. The notion of the Fatherhood of God, for instance, emerged in the circumstances of the Hebrew people who, especially in early, patriarchal times, had no opportunity for deep philosophical reflection but expressed their religious perceptions in terms of their own experience and their own society.

The Christian Way developed out of Judaism in such a manner as to make such symbolic modes ineradicable from it. They have become part of its poetry. To tamper with them now is like trying to abolish the Englishness of Shakespeare by rendering him officially and definitively into Italian or Chinese. Of course you can translate (up to a point), although translation notoriously traduces the original, and you can certainly write learned commentary in other languages and with other modes of symbolizing. This is indeed what happened long ago, of course, when Christianity was subjected to philosophical analysis in terms of the intellectual climate of the Mediterranean world. The basic poetic symbols for the expression of Christian faith, however, have never been nor ever should be changed. Nevertheless, they have been and they ought always to be *illumined* by new symbols.

The wisdom of the doctrine of karma needs christening. That the term *karma* is an import from India should cause no misgiving to Christians, for many of the most hallowed terms in Christian theology are imports from a variety of ancient lands including, for instance, Persia. The fact that the Fatherhood of God and other central Christian concepts are recognized by and derived from other religions has never been and certainly ought not to be any reason for a Christian's rejecting them. Only if the karmic principle could be shown to be contrary to what Christians have all along tried to express as the core of their faith could they be justified in repudiating it.

Far from this being the case, the karmic principle provides an apposite expression of the heart of the teaching of Jesus. That is not to say that all Christian teaching can be reduced to it. Of course not. It is nevertheless a cardinal principle in the Christian outlook.

The karmic principle, in summing up one crucially important aspect of biblical teaching, exhibits the nature of our satisfaction in "working out" our own salvation "in fear and trembling" (Philippians 2.12). We are co-workers with the Lord who has redeemed us and made our salvation possible. The principle goes far beyond the moral law, encompassing as it does the concept of the divine suffering that lies at the heart of the creative process. It is both God's law and God's love. It is the love that moves the sun and the other stars (*l'amor che muove il sole e l'altre stelle*) in Dante's famous line: the love that entails infinite sacrifice and whose generosity knows no bounds. That such a principle should seem foreign or fearsome to anyone claiming to be Christian seems sad indeed, for as a convenient means of expressing the core of the Christian outlook on life and the essence of Christian hope, pithily summing it up in a single word, surely no term in the history of religion is more ripe for christening than is this ancient Sanskrit word *karma*. As the English mystic, Mother Julian of Norwich, reminds us, no one has ever promised us that we should not be subjected to suffering and dismay; we are promised only that we shall not be overcome. That is precisely what follows from the principle of karma.

This principle can be obscured in Christianity as it is by habits of intellectual sloth and by that kind of literalism (often claiming to be "fundamentalism") that is typical of that fundamentally irreligious outlook that is only too common in all the religions of the world and produces such travesties of them, not least of Christian faith. Against it also stand ignorance, thoughtlessness, and above all the vested interests of institutionalisms that feed upon such sad conditions. Recognition of the karmic principle and meditation upon it undermine the power that officers of institutional religion like to exercise. Notorious to all serious students of religion is the fact that there are important elements and agencies in all organized religion that encourage the votaries to cling desperately to all that fosters dependence on the Church. Part of the attractiveness of karmic doctrine lies in the fact that it is a bulwark against the pseudo-theologies in the Church that give lip service to independent spirituality while surreptitiously championing non-think. Only those with such vested interests have anything to fear from a spread of the recognition of the karmic principle, which so many thoughtful people everywhere have for long already recognized, by whatever name they call it and under whatever theological terminology they conceive it.

To those who have not been fully aware of karma, the discovery of it is superabundantly liberating. While they need not repudiate the background in which they were nurtured, an appreciation of karma should enable them to develop their spirituality with none of the bitterness that some feel when they sally forth on their own for the first time. On the contrary, it should make spiritual growth rapid and independence lasting and secure while at the same time enhancing rather than diminishing that love for the Church that guided and protected them as a mother guides toddlers before they can walk on their own.

The Hebrew Bible is rooted in the Torah or Law. Law, however, is no mere collection of statutes or commandments; it is a revelation of God's nature, exhibiting an aspect of karma. When the laws of Hammurabi, engraved on a diorite stele, were found in 1902 at Susa in Elam, scholars noted how closely this extrabiblical collection of laws paralleled the biblical law set forth in the Pentateuch (Torah) and traditionally attributed to Moses. By that time the Mosaic authorship of these first five books of the Hebrew Bible had been for long repudiated by critical scholars of the Bible. Since then various other extrabiblical collections of laws from the ancient Middle East have been discovered, predating by many centuries the earliest biblical compilations and even the earliest date that might be ascribed with any plausibility to the traditional but shadowy figure of Moses. Abundant evidence is now available besides the Hammurabi stele, which is now housed in the Louvre in Paris, showing that the biblical collection of laws, including what has come down to us as the Decalogue or "Ten Commandments," had antecedents among other neighboring peoples and is rooted in a long history of ancient legislation.

What is peculiar to the biblical tradition as developed by the Hebrew people is the notion that the law (the Torah, as they called it) is the expression of the will of God. No strict parallel is known to exist for this unique attitude of the Hebrews, among whom the law became a sacred obligation under a covenant with God. This unique attitude is particularly striking after the Exile (587 B.C.E.) when the Torah, no longer the legislation of an independent society, became in Judaism the guide to life, the ethical lodestone for the chosen people of God. The use of the term *tôrah* as applied to the whole law and eventually to the Pentateuch itself is to be found before the Exile; but after the Exile the Torah comes to be identified with wisdom (Wisdom of Sirach 24;39.1-11). Some rabbis went so far as to venerate the law as having existed before creation, recognizing it not only as given by God but as *identifiable with the moral perfection of God.* By the time of

Jesus, the Pharisees, adopting such an attitude toward the
Torah, surrounded it with a fence of oral tradition that they
accounted second in sanctity to the Torah itself. They sought
to achieve by this means the perfect observance of the Torah.

Jesus contended that the Pharisees had become so trapped
in the maze of legislation and legalistic observance, which
included 613 distinct commandments, that they had lost
sight of righteousness itself, the righteousness that is at the
heart of the universe because it is at the heart of God. It was
this righteousness, this essential holiness, that formulations
of the law had been designed to express. Indeed they had
attained some measure of success in the expression of it. The
worst service one could do to those who had tried so to formu-
late the moral law of God was to worship the formulation and
fail to see what it was that was being formulated.

The karmic principle behind the Torah and all other such
formulations has also been expressed, of course, in phrases
such as "You reap what you sow." No such neat formulation,
however, gives more than a very limited, one-sided view of
the principle itself. To be sure, karma does mean that one
reaps the moral effect of everything one thinks and says and
does. Yet it also means that, in the spiritual realm no less
than in the physical one, duty is not imposed on us by a lawgiver, divine or human, but is written into the nature of the
spiritual dimension of being as surely as is gravity written
into the nature of our planetary system. It is not merely a
restriction; it also sustains us. Unless we see the comprehensiveness of karma, it will seem to us like a stern, narrow-
minded schoolmaster who cramps us at every point,
conforming us to an ineluctable, drearily unchangeable rule.
On the contrary, karma is also the principle of spiritual
liberation. It provides the conditions for the attainment of
our individual freedom.

How can that which constrains be that which liberates?
How can that which imprisons me be that which sets me
free? A commonplace in the scientific study of nature provides
a clue. When automobiles were first designed, the designers
went on following the style of the old horse-drawn carriage,

as though the only difference between the old vehicle and the new was that the new was (as it was indeed at first sometimes called) a horseless carriage. The early models were rather clumsy and now look a bit funny. They were as they were precisely because of the misconception that they were simply the old carriage without the horse. When eventually they came to be streamlined, they better obeyed nature, being accordingly more efficient as well as smoother and pleasanter to the eye. Nature must be obeyed, for we have to work within the limits she prescribes; but in obeying her we discover our own individual freedom, which is closed to us so long as we are resisting her. So it is in the spiritual realm of being. So long as we refuse to recognize our karmic situation we are awkward, maladroit, ungainly, ineffective. This state of affairs is symptomatic of what the Christian theologians call sin. By yielding to divine Being we become more like what a spiritual being ought to be, knowing the joy of spiritual liberation. An old Anglican collect calls service to God "perfect freedom" (the original Latin form in the Gelasian Sacramentary is *cui servire regnare est*: "whom to serve is to reign"), which well expresses this paradoxical aspect of the karmic principle. Acceptance of karma does not mean a mere passive submission to the outcome of our past misdeeds; it means, rather, recognizing the nature and scope of what we have to work with. Only in view of all this may we usefully talk of the karmic principle as a "law," and if we do we ought never to confuse it with any formulation whatsoever, for while it encompasses many formulations it transcends them all.

We all start life with assets and handicaps of one sort or another. Some of the handicaps are peculiarly grievous and have a high degree of visibility, such as a physical deformity or a debilitating disease, a speech impediment or a defective vision, grinding poverty or a loveless environment. Any observer will detect such disabilities at once. But we may also inherit psychological dispositions, libidinal tendencies, disturbances of the spirit, that handicap us in other ways. Our whole task in life is to liberate ourselves from the negative karmic heritage we have acquired and take advantage of our opportunities and abilities. The first thing we have to know about this enterprise is that it must be accomplished in full view of the conditions provided us. Our task in life is like that of a farmer who, energetic and hardworking though he be, will get nowhere till he takes account of the climate, the soil, the terrain, with which he has to work. He must work within the scope of what he has to work with. He will get nowhere even with the most sophisticated farming implements and soil conditioners unless he first takes into account the conditions he has to face and to improve. So the recognition of the nature and scope of the problems and challenges that confront us in our karmic heritage is the first and indispensable step toward their solution.

What follows, however, is crucial. For it is precisely in becoming aware of the conditions people face that many of them take fright, becoming spiritually paralyzed. Like a stage-struck actor whose tongue cleaves to the roof of his mouth as he tries to speak his lines, or like a telephone linesman who develops vertigo as he climbs the pole, many a person on seeing what life demands freezes at the sight. The more one tries, the worse one becomes. It is not a question of trying harder; it is a question, rather, of coming to terms with the conditions, which is infinitely more difficult than "trying hard" and yet infinitely easier once one "gets the knack of it." Sometimes people enjoin the victim to relax; but relaxing is easier said than done and in any case much more is needed.

The way out is variously described. Zen masters might call it a *satori*, a kind of jolt to shake the psyche out of a bind. Churchmen might call it "help from on high" or the intervention of divine grace. We shall see more about this in our next chapter. Whatever it is, help issues from the karmic principle itself in another of its many aspects. The situation is such that it cannot be cured by "more of the same" any more than, in sawing into a log of wood, we shall get out of a bind by sawing harder. We must disengage the saw and start again at a different angle so as to make what woodsmen call a "V" or an "A." Often, however, the situation is such that we cannot get out of the bind by ourselves any more than we could get out of a sinking sand by struggling harder. We need "help from on high." Karma has a vertical as well as a horizontal dimension. That is to say, it encompasses help that comes to us from beyond as well as what we do by our own efforts. As the law of the moral realm it affects us at every point. From our human perspective karmic circumstance often seems full of paradox. Even as our karma seems to hinder us it helps; even as it helps it seems to hinder. It comes as a challenge to our will, stark and uncompromising; yet at the same time it is the means through which our wills can be set free and go into effective action.

Karma, then, is indeed what is celebrated in the Judaeo-Christian tradition in which the Law of the Lord (the Torah) is acclaimed as "perfect, new life for the soul" (Psalm 19.7, Jerusalem Bible); but it is far more than anything commonly understood as law or even moral principle. Karma is the very nature of divine Being itself. The nearer we come into union with God through mystical knowledge, the more we see how much larger and roomier is the mansion that is now our home. Yet, although we are freed by understanding of the karmic principle, we are at the same time constrained to make greater and greater sacrifices. For divine Being is infinitely free and yet (as Thomas Aquinas puts it) "cannot act contrary to his own nature" which is essentially and eternally creative and creativity entails infinitely sacrificial love.

Freedom and love are at the heart of divine Being and therefore at the heart of the karmic law. All that we can call law is only the husk—whether the moral law (expressed in a "Golden Rule" or a "categorical imperative") or the "laws" of Nature. True, the glory of divine Being shines through even to the outer shell that is the nearest that many people come to seeing God; but as God is greater than any formulation of him ever can be. so the karmic principle that governs all our relations to God is larger than anything we can ever attribute to it. In our next chapter we shall see how the concept of grace reflects awareness of this overwhelming glory in the nature of divine Being.

4

Grace Surprises

"Grace" has been pushed into an entirely wrong position; we use grace to slough off the requirement of the law. This is meaningless and unchristian!

S. Kierkegaard, *Papirer*

No one can seriously study evolutionary theories such as those that issued in the work of Darwin and his followers without being confronted with one prevailing puzzle, to which the nineteenth-century evolutionists were forced to give much attention: how are we to account for and interpret the "missing links" in the process? For the process, whatever it is, is patently not one of steady progression as of a kettle in which the temperature of the water gradually reaches boiling point under the influence of the steady flame. On the contrary, it looks rather as though the flame were periodically stopped and then suddenly spurted forth with unparalleled power, raising the temperature in an astonishingly short time, then relapsing into a mere back-burner jet, only to burst forth again into a flame so powerful that the kettle almost immediately whistles in a shriek of triumph. It is easy enough, for instance, to see how anthropoid are some of our simian ancestors; it is difficult, however, to see how the leap from their level to that of even the earlier forms of man could take place without leaving traces of the process. That evolutionary advance should take millions of years need not astonish us; indeed, we might well find room for astonishment that it takes place as quickly as that, when we consider the tremendous complexity of biological organization that is accomplished between the lowest forms of life and that of even a cat or a dog. What is remarkable is not the length of the process but that it does not occur, as we might expect, in a steady flow.

It seems that a certain balance must be reached before an organism is capable of the leap to a definitely new and higher stage of evolution. Moreover, it must make a "decision," a "choice" that involves foregoing one direction of growth in favor of another; for instance, to grow wings or fins. Not only must it presumably be ready to make the choice; it must be capable of carrying it out. What makes it possible for it to do so now when for perhaps a thousand centuries it has merely been marking time in an evolutionary rut?

Although an organism attains its evolutionary development on its own, by its own effort, it is not alone. It is not struggling in a vacuum. Other agents are present in the vortex of life, so that when it is ready to be drawn upward by them it can be so drawn. Even at such levels there is a creative force behind the evolutionary process that draws everything upwards whenever it is capable of being so drawn. Even in biological development in the individual life of an organism we can see this force at work: the little bird flutters till it is ready to fly; the bud hesitates till it is ready to bloom; the little boy or girl lingers expectantly till he or she is ready to mate. Evolution is a process of drawing out. Creation consists in the drawing out of what is ready to be drawn.

If it is so at the biological level, we may expect to find some counterpart of it at the higher levels of consciousness. And so indeed we do. As an organism can remain settled in a biological rut for many millennia, the spiritual development of a self at the human level can remain stagnant for many lifetimes while its karmic balance is being worked out, and then, with a mercurial speed, it suddenly bursts into bloom. Some people are late bloomers. Like the tortoise in the fable, they overtake the hare. The karmic principle of spiritual balance is always there; but along with it is the ever-vigilant creative force, the divine principle, awaiting the opportunity to lift the struggling, sinking soul out of the morass. Whenever the soul in its struggle has matured sufficiently to restore its karmic balance, the divine principle of creative love is there, seeking out that soul and drawing it upwards toward those higher reaches whither it has always been bound but has failed to attain sooner because of karmic imbalance. The situation often has become desperate just before the arrival of the "moment of truth." It is as with an alcoholic who is on the brink of disaster when, in the nick of time, he or she makes a Herculean effort of decision and is then rendered capable of being drawn out of his plight and into a realm of joy and peace.

This is indeed precisely what is celebrated in all religious conversion. The convert, sinking fast into the mud of his own making, cries out in anguish. As he does so he becomes capable of being drawn upward not only to safety but to new life. Without the acknowledgement of such a benign presence, such a creative principle, the notion of a spiritual evolution would indeed be entirely unintelligible. The Christian doctrine of grace, in which one is, in C. S. Lewis's felicitous phrase, "surprised by joy," is a peculiarly emphatic expression of this aspect of the universal love of God. As most of the great religions of the world recognize the significance of conversion, so most have counterparts of one sort or another to the notion of grace.

Religious concepts corresponding closely to that of grace as developed in Christian scripture and tradition occur, for example, in the Pure Land schools of Amida Buddhism in Japan. Honen (1133-1212) and his disciple Shinran (1173-1262) both emphatically taught the sinfulness of humanity and the need of salvation through the grace of Amida. Honen distinguished two ways of salvation: (1) the way of meditation in one's own power (*jiriki*), which he called the difficult way, and (2) the way of dependence on the mercy of Amida Buddha (*tariki*), which he called the easy way. The contrast much resembles that which is made in Christian tradition between salvation by works and salvation by grace and in Hindu tradition between *karma-yoga* and *bhakti-yoga.* According to Honen, man is helpless by himself. Although theoretically he ought to be able to work out his own salvation, he is so depraved that he cannot in fact do so; he needs the help of another and he must find this by looking to Amida and finding in him the grace to be saved. Shinran developed his master's views in a theology centered upon the notion of salvation by grace.

Christians need not be particularly astonished to find such a counterpart to the concept of grace in some forms of Buddhism; the notion was already present in the Hebrew tradition Christians inherit and in which Jesus himself was nurtured. The notion that God shows favor is firmly rooted in the Hebrew Bible. Yahweh shows favor, for instance, by giving people children (Genesis 33.5) and prosperity (Genesis 33.11). In Trito-Isaiah we are told that Yahweh says to his people: "Long before they call I shall answer; before they stop speaking I shall have heard" (Isaiah 65.24). That God takes the initiative in saving man is certainly not alien to Hebrew thought; nor is the notion that the faithful Israelite puts himself wholeheartedly and unreservedly in the benevolent hand of God, whose lovingkindness is ever ready to be poured out upon those who trust in him.

Indeed, the notion that there are two ingredients in salvation is widespread in the religions of humankind. On the one hand, I must stand on my own two feet, walking in solitary independence, struggling to find my way to heaven; on the other hand, I must recognize my extreme weakness and willingly acknowledge my total dependence on whatever focus of spiritual strength I can find. My industry is good, but no work-righteousness can provide the whole answer. It may even cause me to choke in my own pride. My arduous toil may lead only to weariness and a sense of futility. So when I hear the voice of the Master with promise of much-needed strength to bear me up, I listen eagerly. If he sends me a rope to rescue me, I grasp it gratefully. Yet that can never be the end of the story. For, being saved, I must now work out my salvation. The various religions express this theme, each in its own way, each recognizing the antinomy. The solution, however, is variously presented.

Since the concept of grace and the divine initiative in human salvation is so strongly emphasized in all strands of Christian thought, although in some more than in others, the rest of this chapter will focus upon Christian presentations of the principle. The principle is, however, universal and its application can be seen wherever men and women are influenced by profound conversion experiences of any kind, even those that are not necessarily dubbed religious in conventional usage.

We have seen that the Christian theological concept of grace has Hebrew antecedents. It appears in the Old Testament in the noun *ḥēn*, "favor," and the verb *ḥānan*, "to show (or bestow) favor." In the New Testament, however, the word *charis*, with its overtones of bounty, generosity, and well-being, acquires such extreme prominence that it becomes a key word, even a technical term, being identified with the Good News (the Gospel) itself. It is used habitually in salutations in the epistles where it is often conjoined with the traditional greeting of peace. It is the very principle of Christian life and action. Stephen, the first martyr to the Christian cause, is said to have been full of grace and power (Acts 6.8). Paul repeatedly speaks of his function in the Church as a grace that he has received and that he must pass on to others (Romans 1.5; 12.3; 15.15; I Corinthians 3.10; 15.10; Galatians 2.9). Grace issues in good works (II Corinthians 8.1). Grace comes directly from Christ and acts mystically in the soul of the recipient.

Although the subject of grace became the occasion of endlessly acrimonious controversy in the history of Christian theology, it has always been acknowledged as a central concept. A cognate term, *charisma*, has been anglicized and suggests a personality endowed with unique openness and charm such as cannot be learned or acquired as one learns chemistry or acquires fluency in a language. It is a gift that transforms the whole being of the recipient at the most radical level. The glowing joy so evident in Paul's use of the term in his letters is reflected in the traditional liturgical use of phrases such as "The grace of the Lord Jesus Christ be with you all," which are used in all the great liturgies of the Church. Apart from grace, Christian teaching is meaningless. In practice it may be often a mere shadow of the reality; neverthless, its centrality is at least formally recognized.

The doctrine of grace was formulated early in the history of Christian thought. Tertullian, in the second century, was probably the first to present a formulation of it as a theological concept. He represents it as the divine energy at work in the human soul. Perhaps it might have been better had that been left as the last word on the subject, since surely it well represents the essence of what the concept of grace is intended to symbolize. In fact, however, from the early fifth century, when the notorious controversy between Augustine and Pelagius on the subject of grace occurred, theological controversy about the nature and operation of grace and its relation to the freedom of the will became as complex as it was acrimonious and after more than a millenium was still unresolved. The problem as it appeared in the Pelagian controversy was essentially this: Christianity is rendered meaningless apart from a recognition of the reality of human freedom and responsibility, yet so overwhelming is the grace of God that one must ask what can be left of freedom when God, in the total abandon of his infinite love, pours forth the divine energy with which he captivates the soul.

Augustine was so impressed by his personal sense of unworthiness in his being chosen by God and of his becoming the recipient of such abundant and wholly unmerited divine favor that he found it difficult not to conclude that the divine Being had simply taken possession of him in such a way that he had no choice left but to go whither the divine energy drove him. Yet in his *De libero arbitrio* he treated of the freedom of choice that the individual has, taking it very seriously indeed. Christian thought and Christian experience seemed at odds: on the one hand, there must be freedom of choice; on the other, the most profound and moving experience was of being simply pursued and captured by the relentless and irresistible love of God. Pelagius, by contrast, emphasized the role of human freedom. The Church in the long run officially sided with Augustine. Unofficially, however, Pelagian influence enormously affected popular religious practice throughout the Middle Ages, whatever the theologians might say.

The sense of having been overtaken by God, so strong in Paul, in Luther, and in innumerable other great figures in Christian history, is so impressive that the problem must not be underestimated. The recipient of grace has an overpowering sense of having been steeped and bathed in the boundless and sanctifying energy of God, despite the extreme unworthiness he or she feels in having been singled out for such special favor. The celebrated exclamation, "There but for the grace of God go I," attributed to John Bradford, John Bunyan, and John Wesley, is an expression of a sentiment widely felt by many less famous persons in Christian history. The problem is a theological counterpart of the age-old philosophical problem of determinism and free choice. How is it to be resolved?

A paradigm is to be found in the Gospel parable of the talents (Matthew 25.14-30). If you, being a generous and rich person, give me, a poor down-and-out, a large sum of money, affording me a unique opportunity to make a start in business, and if I then make a great success out of that opportunity, surely I must be an ungrateful wretch if I should fail to pay tribute to you daily in my thoughts. Without you I could not possibly have taken even the first step toward the success I have achieved. How could I dare in your presence to boast of my success? Yet did you in any way diminish my freedom? Of course not. On the contrary, you enlarged my capacity for it and stimulated my exercise of that capacity. Again, how can I ever repay the kindergarten teacher who first roused my intellectual interest? Think of what I owe her. Yet did she eradicate in me the need or the desire to work? By no means. On the contrary, it was she who first so enlivened my mind as to induce in me the desire to do so. She might even be called

the cause of the ferment in my mind that led to my free choice
of devoting hour after hour, day after day, year after year, of
arduous toil in the pursuit of learning. Can she in any way at
all be said to have curtailed my freedom? Of course not.
Instead, she opened up to me vistas that would otherwise
have been closed to me. By constraining me to look at a
larger panorama she gave me not less liberty but more. So,
then, in the most profound way of all does God give me new
and boundless opportunities as pure gift, as sheer favor, as
amazing grace. The divine grace, irresistible though it be to
those who are the happy recipients of it, in no way restricts
but much more enlarges my capacity for freedom.

These are the kinds of consideration we should bear in
mind when, with a view to the christening of karma, we
naturally raise the question: "What can Christian grace have
to do with karma, the principle that is the eternal moral law,
the principle of duty, the balance that lies at the core of all
things and is so fundamental, so inexorable, that not even
the most basic physical laws we know of can be called so
immutable?" How can grace, so seemingly arbitrary and
suprarational an outpouring of divine energy, be squared
with a principle such as karma?

The answer is simple. No squaring has to be done or could
be done. For the moral-law aspect of the karmic principle is
but one side of this marvellously multifaceted doctrine of the
Ancient Wisdom. If, as is central to Christian faith, the cosmic
energy has as its source the inexhaustible riches of the infinite
love of God, then karma, the moral law that governs the working of that cosmic energy, is inseparable from the divine
benevolence and love at its source. We, accustomed as we are
to the all-too-human limitations within which our lives are
lived, tend to think of duty as a stern task-master and of the
eternal moral law as a rigorous and unbending machine. Our
traditional symbol of justice is indeed a pair of scales operated
by a blindfold lady so detached from her work that she cannot
even see what she is doing. The symbol expresses well enough
that detachment from prejudice and emotional sentiment
that administrators of the law ought constantly to maintain.

We rightly hail it as a noble emblem of our great legal institutions. When, however, we go on to interpret the nature of karma in such terms, we grievously traduce it. The justice of God is not at all blind or mechanistic. It needs no courts of equity to redress imperfect judgments. All through the moral law that is a central aspect of the divine nature runs that eternal disposition of creative love at the heart of God. Law and love are so interwoven in God that the one can never be found without the other. They belong to one another as do the inside and the outside of a bottle.

Grace flows eternally from God. God is gracious Being. We are constantly within the sphere of its blessed influence. So constant is the presence of divine grace that we are generally not acutely conscious of it. We bask in it as we bask in the sunshine; we breathe it as we breathe the air. Only at special times and in special circumstances do we attain a sharp awareness of it at work in the depths of our own being. We feel a sudden rush of its power within us, a sudden quickening of our consciousness, a heightening of our self-awareness, a sense of our participation in Being itself that the mystics call union with God. The sluice gates of our soul are opened and grace pours in, overwhelming us with its beneficent power. Coming to us in utter humility, there is in it no hint of the arrogance that is so characteristic of the exercise of human power or the bestowal of human favor. Despite all the controversies in the history of Christian thought about the nature of the operation of grace in the human soul, all Christians have been agreed that it is overwhelming. It makes the recipient feel the puniness of his own efforts and the grandeur and magnanimity of the favor that has been lavished upon him.

Paul heard Christ tell him: "My grace is sufficient for thee; for my strength is made perfect in weakness" (II Corinthians 12.9). It is the universal testimony of Christian experience that the impact of grace is most felt and its power most efficaciously appropriated when one's spirit is at a low ebb. When we are most aware of our own weakness, we most vividly apprehend the divine strength.

So, then, grace is built into the karmic principle. According to Thomist teaching *gratia non tollit naturam sed perficit*: grace does not take away nature but perfects it. (*Summa Theologiae*, I, 1, 8 ad 2). Grace is always available to us, but we do not always appropriate it. Even as we grasp the basic principle of the moral law, that one reaps what one sows, we have a tendency to detach it from the gracious purpose of God and to regard it as an inexorable operation of justice as in the eye-for-an-eye, tooth-for-a-tooth formula. Karma, however, is not merely more than that; it is ill represented in any such way. The reason is simple. Karma is the moral law of divine Being, which is itself gracious. God's justice and God's mercy work together. In the operation of the karmic law we are not punished as by an angry dictator or vengeful conqueror. On the contrary, we are corrected as by a loving parent. The correction presents us with difficulties to be faced but at the same time with opportunities to be enjoyed. The karmic principle is nothing if not creative. It is, like the evolutionary process itself, "God's way of doing things." It is nothing if not a law of love. Sometimes, indeed, our major difficulty lies in our being unwilling to accept the fact that we are forgiven. Love is difficult for the loveless to accept.

Virginia Hanson quotes what Joseph Campbell writes of a great Peruvian deity: "The meaning is that the grace that pours into the universe through the sun door is the same as the energy of the bolt that annihilates and is itself indestructible; the delusion-shattering light of the Imperishable is the same as the light that creates."[1] She rightly concludes that karma and grace "are, in fact, but two aspects of the same law."[2]

Talking of karma as a law is, indeed, to use a figure that may be misleading. As we have seen, it is the working out of a principle of balance and harmony. To talk as we commonly

1. J. Campbell, *The Hero With a Thousand Faces*, Bollingen Series XVII (New York: Pantheon Books, 1968), p. 146.

2. Virginia Hanson, "The Other Face of Karma," in V. Hanson and R. Stewart (eds.), *Karma* (Wheaton, IL: Theosophical Publishing House, 1981), p. 160.

do of "the laws of physics" is recognized to be misleading,
since what are called laws of physics are enunciations of
principles that physicists find in nature, such as the "law" of
gravity and the "second law" of thermodynamics. So in the
spiritual realm the concept of karma expresses a principle
that we find there: a principle one aspect of which *reminds* us
of such a "law" in physics but reminds us also of what religious
people, speaking out of the depth of their experience, call favor
or grace. If God is anything like what the Bible and Christian
tradition say he is, then he is not constrained to act in certain
ways or to decree according to certain pre-established edicts
as a judge is constrained to administer the law as it has been
determined by the legislative branch of government. As an
old school of Protestant theologians would have said: God's
wrath is his mercy and his mercy is his wrath.

In the past two hundred years no thinker has been at once
more profoundly Christian and more sharply critical of
popular Christianity than was the Danish writer Søren Aaby
Kierkegaard (1813-1855), whose prolific writings were all but
ignored till some seventy years after his death when they
began to be immensely influential both among theologians
and among existentialist philosophers. On the subject in
hand he is characteristically perceptive. He writes that "just
because grace is shown to me and I am reprieved, precisely
in this lies the requirement to exert myself all the more." He
cites Luther as expressing a similar view. Again he asks: "Is it
Christianity's intention to eliminate striving by means of
grace? No, Christianity simply wants to have the law fulfilled,
if possible, by means of grace .... Christianity's intention is:
now as never before under the law we shall see what a man
can achieve. But instead of this we have used 'grace' to prevent
acting. Instead of 'grace' as the basis of courage and mobility
for action it is applied in such a way that it even causes an
unnatural obstruction; it is applied in such a way that by
means of grace one sinks deeper and deeper into softness and
effeminacy in order to require continually more and more
grace. We continually run across this kind of thing: Since we
are all saved by grace anyway, why should I exert myself;

anything could happen if I were promptly to begin making an effort . . . ."

Kierkegaard's relentless satire dramatically brings home the demanding character of grace and its intimate connection with, indeed its inseparability from, duty and law. "With the help of 'grace' the point has now been reached, especially within Protestantism, of smuggling Christianity completely out of everything. We are all saved by grace—the matter is decided once for all—and thereupon we arrange our lives according to the best paganism. The intention of Christianity was to introduce 'grace' into life in order to transform all life." His bitterness against ecclesiastical parodies of the Christian Way rises to a crescendo as he exclaims: "But this is the frightful deception which permeates all Christendom— that human authority has appropriated 'grace' and now makes a business of it, at times sells it for money, then again wins the amiability and esteem of men by confirming them in cheerful enjoyment of life—for, after all, there is grace. No, no! This is the Christian rigorousness which must not be altered—where grace is concerned each man must address himself to God, be alone with him, and no man should have the audacity to want to be an intermediate authority between God and another man."[3]

Surely these passages speak for themselves. Kierkegaard lived in an age in which the term *karma* was scarcely known in the milieu of European scholars. Yet although he could not have been thinking of the karmic principle in the terms that have become familiar to us westerners in the past hundred years or so, he was not only clearly delineating it but showing, in these passages and elsewhere in his writings, the inseparability of grace and law.

The abuse of the concept of grace in popular Christianity has fostered untold evils. Although people who in one way or another have understood the demands of the Christian Way and have made serious attempts to follow the precepts

3. Kierkegaard, *Papirer*. These excerpts are from *Søren Kierkegaard's Journals and Papers*, Vol. 2, edited and translated by H. V. and E. H. Hong (Bloomington: Indiana University Press, 1970), pp. 166ff.

enjoined upon those who engage in that enterprise, a remarkable number of professing Christians are apparently content to accept almost any "theological boilerplate" that the officers of their Church choose to impose upon them, accepting even the notion that no matter how personally unworthy, ignorant, and avaricious a bishop or other church officer may be, he remains nevertheless the appointed channel of "grace" to whose words all faithful Christians have the duty to attend. Such a travesty of the teaching and work of Jesus Christ does not merely alienate intelligent people from religion of every kind; it produces a peculiarly vicious kind of hypocrisy, the kind that flagrantly disregards truth for the sake of dogma known to be contrary to the mind of Christ no less than of other great masters of spirituality in human history. Setting grace and law in opposition as though they were mutually incompatible is the cause of immense moral mischief, including a widespread devaluation of the Christian Way in the popular mind.

Grace and the moral law hang together because grace, far from superseding or destroying freedom of choice, provides the means whereby individual freedom can be attained on a far grander scale. It is as constantly available to the human spirit as is the impetus toward spiritual evolution, but we are notoriously prone to block and otherwise resist it. When seemingly favored or specially chosen individuals receive and appropriate grace, it comes to them within and indeed as an aspect of the karmic principle itself, which does not by any means exclude generosity, sympathy, and love. Everyone who has genuinely experienced the gift of grace knows that it is nothing if not the beginning of a new freedom in the soul, bringing in its train a deeper understanding of the moral law such as had been hitherto beyond the recipient's ken. Grace enlarges me and my apprehension of the karmic principle of which it is so singularly welcome a strand.

The novelty and the liberation that the Christian claims to find in Jesus Christ is in fact no more irreconcilable with the pervasive principle of karma than is a doctrine of free choice irreconcilable with the indisputable fact that we do face circumstances not of our own choosing, circumstances that are simply given to us as is a hand at bridge. Freedom of choice is indeed meaningless where there is nothing to choose from. You and I get the same play dough, but we use it very differently and out of it we make very different things. Karma determines the way the spiritual dimension works; it does not determine how I make it work for me or how I fail to do so.

I have said that we both start with the same play dough, but to this may be raised the obvious objection: not at all, for your play dough package seems to have provided you with natural talents, a brilliant mind, a healthy physical constitution, and a comfortable and loving home, while mine included only a meager talent, a pedestrian mind, a weak physical constitution, and a homeless and loveless poverty. We cannot, then, be said to have started with anything like the same play dough, for it would seem that someone has been already working on yours, making it beautiful and fine before you even opened the package, while mine seems to have been vandalized before I got it. The reason, of course, is that the play dough with which we start, the play dough in which the karmic law is ever at work, indeed has been already worked on. You had already worked on yours and I on mine. For the karmic law works along with the reincarnationist principle, apart from which it would be unintelligible. We have both started with the play dough with which we finished in our last life. The play dough is the same stuff, but yours and mine have been differently treated. We are equal in the sense that we are both subject to precisely the same moral law; we are very unequal in the sense that you may be much more experienced both in coping with its demands and in transcending its constraints. For although karma entails a principle of restraint as part of its nature, no less essential to its nature is its capacity to provide liberation.

Our stage in spiritual evolution, which is governed by the karmic law and attained by our own free choice within the workings of that law, is what has determined the kind of play dough we get. Hampered as I am by the burdens and restrictions I have created for myself, I am also freed through every noble thought I have ever conceived, every compassionate and helpful word I have ever spoken, and above all by every good deed I have ever done. I clear my own evolutionary path in the act of extricating myself from the effects of my negative and destructive thoughts and words and deeds, and in so clearing my way I create opportunities that I lacked and open doors that had been closed to me. Through attunement to the karmic principle I speed up the process of spiritual evolution in which I am engaged. My play dough melts more easily in my hands, enabling me to do more and better with it.

The Christian claims to have found in Christ the perfect catalyst, the catalyst uniquely suited to the liberating process. He or she can then see no need to look elsewhere. When the physician's treatment is working well, why seek another? Only when one is in doubt does one seek another opinion. The Christian entertains many doubts on all sorts of questions, but if he or she finds that a radical change has actually taken place in the development of his spiritual life, no doubt can be entertained. When one's sickness has gone, the pain has subsided, and weariness has given place to a sense of well-being and a flow of abundant energy and radiant vitality, one may still harbor many a doubt on many a topic, but on the subject of the transformation in one's health doubt is impossible.

The Christian's affirmation of the uniqueness of the role of Jesus Christ in redemption springs, then, from personal experience. What the Christian affirms is an existential truth such as is recorded of the blind man in the Gospel: "I only know that I was blind and now I can see" (John 9.25). From there the Christian *may* go on to metaphysical assertions about the role of Jesus Christ in the redemption of humankind, of the cosmos, of the elect, and so forth, but the ground of the metaphysical speculation must rest in the last resort on his or her own personal experience. That does not mean that the metaphysical conclusions may not be warranted (at least as warranted as any metaphysical conclusion ever can be); it means only that personal experience is the basis of the metaphysical argument.

In saying that Jesus Christ is, to use classical Protestant language, "the full and final revelation of God," the Christian is saying, in effect: "I have found it so, having travelled far and wide along the paths mapped out by prophets and sages." The prophets and sages may have been men such as Gautama and Moses or they may have been merely the Christian's own family and teachers and friends. The conviction can relate only to what he or she has in fact experienced and how he or she has felt compelled to interpret that experience.

Over the course of years the interpretation may be revised. Our understanding of spiritual events does not come complete and neatly packaged with the event itself. Our understanding develops with the impact of the event on our lives and with the influence of our lives on the experience of the event. One does not see all of a tree at first sight; nor does one grasp a symphony in its entirety on first hearing or a great novel on first reading. What it means to say that Jesus Christ is the "full and final revelation of God" and that he has a "unique role in my redemption" does not come in an instant. The event in my life, with the leap it provokes and the readjustment it entails, has far too much in it to be appreciated all at once. Yet all the way through the process of spiritual development that has been begun, the Christian is saying: "What more could I need? I have 'the Way, the Truth, and the Life.' "

Some more will be said on grace in Chapter 12. Meanwhile, we are now in a position to consider the specific question: can the karmic principle be legitimately christened within the framework of historic Christian tradition? To this I would say an emphatic yes. The next chapter will therefore be devoted to it before we proceed to a consideration of some of the principal implicates of a spiritual understanding of the evolutionary principle.

5

The Christening of Karma

*Do not imagine that I have come to abolish the
Law or the Prophets. I have not come to abolish
but to complete them.*

Jesus (Matthew 5.17)

The concept of karma, properly understood as specifying a
universal moral principle that entails profound individual
responsibility for one's actions, generally alarms Christians.
That is partly because for various complex reasons reincarnationism with which it is associated has had a bad press in
the history of Christian thought and practice. Despite the
enormous body of literature in which it has appeared in the
West, it still seems to many an alien and essentially Indian
notion, as ill-fitted to a Christian outlook as would be a stupa
or pagoda atop a Gothic church. Apart, however, from such
widespread and perhaps not unnatural prejudices against
the doctrine of karma and reincarnationism (prejudices
already considered), some serious objections are raised by
informed Christians to the proposal that the doctrine of
karma may be with propriety christened as eminently reconcilable with Christian faith, even as that faith is interpreted
by the most orthodox and traditionalist of Christians.

One of the most obvious of such objections is that Christian
faith, being grounded in the recognition of the power of Jesus

70

Christ to save me and, through his death and resurrection, to raise me (my sins notwithstanding) to everlasting life, can have no place for an inexorable moral law such as is implied in the concept of karma. This type of objection is likely to be raised more vehemently among those Christians who account themselves "Protestant" than among those who regard themselves as "Catholics." That this should be so looks at first somewhat paradoxical to those of us who recall that Kant, who has been traditionally revered in Protestant thought and feared by traditionalist Catholic thinkers, argues in the *Critique of Practical Reason* for a view that is almost an exact occidental counterpart of the oriental doctrine of karma. His "categorical imperative" expresses in encapsulated form the basic moral principle at the heart of the universe: duty. Not only is the universe subject to "physical laws" (the law of "the starry heavens above"): it is governed no less inexorably by another law, "the moral law within." This law, according to Kant, operates just as surely as the law of gravity or any other of the so-called "laws of physics." It is I alone, moreover, who am responsible for my actions, as are you for yours. If Kant's ethical teachings could be, as they have been, so palatable to Protestant Christian thought and so acceptable even to Catholic thought (for Catholic objection to his thought was not directed to his ethics but, rather, to his metaphysical skepticism), why should the notion of karma strike such terror in so many Christian hearts?

But let us probe deeper and into canonical Christian Scripture itself. In the Sermon on the Mount, that most venerated collection of the utterances of Jesus, these words are attributed to the Lord himself: "Do not imagine that I have come to abolish the Law or the Prophets. I have come not to abolish but to complete them. I tell you solemnly, till heaven and earth disappear, not one dot, not one little stroke, shall disappear from the Law until its purpose is achieved." (Matthew 5.17f Jerusalem Bible) Jesus is speaking, of course, of the Torah—to Jews still the most sacred part of the Bible. He is saying that the *formulations* of the moral law that is at the heart of all things may be inadequate and so may be improved or enriched; but the Law itself is unchangeable. The law affords, as the psalmist said long before, "perfect, new life for the soul." (Psalm 19.7 Jerusalem Bible) So Jesus goes on: "Therefore, the man who infringes even one of the least of these commandments and teaches others to do the same will be considered the least in the kingdom of heaven; but the man who keeps them and teaches them will be considered great in the kingdom of heaven. For I tell you, if your virtue goes no deeper than that of the scribes and Pharisees, you will never get into the kingdom of heaven." (Matthew 19f Jerusalem Bible) These words leave one in no doubt that no Christian dare pretend to a means of bypassing the moral law which Jesus describes in almost exactly the terms in which one would describe moral implicates of the law of karma.

Why, then, is there so much resistance to the concept of karma and its entailments on the part of Christians? It is not easy to avoid the conclusion that antinomianism (the view that Christians are by grace freed from the need to obey the Law or even to recognize it) is, under various guises and sometimes ingenious disguises, more widespread in the Christian Church than is commonly supposed either within it or outside it. A genuinely deep concern for morality and righteousness cannot be said to be strikingly characteristic either of the leaders of the Church or of the average churchgoer. A passion for justice is certainly no more characteristic of the assemblies of the Church than is a passionate concern for the truth, the absence of which was cited by Lord Russell as his fundamental reason for not being a Christian. Yet every educated Christian must surely know that to talk of grace without the Law is like talking of literature without language. Indeed, it is much worse: it is like talking of love without sacrifice.

What, according to Christian teaching, does Christ do for the Christian? What is the nature of his redemptive work? The answer, however formulated, is essentially this: he puts the Christian in the right way, providing the conditions that make possible his or her salvation. Through faith in Christ the Christian is "justified," that is, "put right," so that it is now possible for him or for her, as before it was not, to be "sanctified," that is, to get out of the bind and make progress in spiritual development. It is the discovery of the aid that Christ provides in this undertaking that causes the Christian to be "surprised by joy." Our evolutionary progress consists indeed in a succession of such surprises.

More serious is the theological objection that, while a program of spiritual evolution attained through reincarnation may be thinkable for Christian believers, it cannot apply to Christ himself who, according to Christian orthodoxy, is "fully God" and "fully man." Since he is God, how can he (as God is conceived in the biblical, Judaeo-Christian tradition) need to progress anywhere at all? Yet if he is also, as Church doctrine insists, "fully man," how can he *not* need to progress, since this is the nature of humanity, and the humanity of Christ, according to orthodox Christian doctrine, must be preserved: to do injury to his humanity is as heterodox as to do injury to his divinity.

Such reflections lead us to a more profound one still. When the early Christians acknowledged Jesus Christ as Lord and Savior of the world, what precisely did they mean? Not only were they far from thinking in terms of possibly inhabited planets on solar systems in distant galaxies, as surely we must think today; their knowledge of planet Earth itself was very limited. Their world extended little beyond the Mediterranean basin.

May not it be that other planets in the trillions of galaxies in the universe have their own counterparts to Jesus Christ, their own unique incarnations of God? A Savior who is "True God and True Man" is fitting indeed for "us men and our salvation," as the Christian creed has it; but suppose there are Martians on Mars. (That Mars might be inhabited by intelligent life seems unlikely, but I use it, of course, as a symbol for one of the many possibilities that might well exist in other solar systems even in our own galaxy.) Jesus would not be fitting for them. They would presumably need a Savior who is True God and True Martian. So then, since we are being for the moment so speculative, suppose that we have just had a radio signal from a planet in some distant galaxy.

We should all be very excited, of course. Christians would be eager to know whether the inhabitants had heard of Jesus Christ. Suppose that they had not but that they had had on their own planet a Being who was the focus of one of their major religions and seemed to function in it precisely the way in which Jesus Christ functions in orthodox Christianity. Would a Christian then be justified in saying, in effect: "No, no, that will not do at all. We must collect money and see that messages are transmitted at once to the other planet to bring them the Good News that the True Savior, the unique Son of God, chose this planet Earth, and that they must therefore acquaint themselves without delay with him and his teaching and accept him as their Savior"? Would a Christian then also feel bound in conscience, the first time that a spaceship went to the other planet, to see that included in the passenger list was a team of missionaries armed with a large supply of Bibles duly translated into whatever language was appropriate to the planetary needs of the new missionary field? Would that spaceship cross one coming in the other direction with emissaries from the other planet addressed to the Patriarch of Constantinople, the Archbishop of Canterbury, the Pope, and the President of the World Council of Churches, in hope of converting their faithful to an allegiance to *their* Savior and Lord?

If that seems absurd, as surely many will perceive it to be, a way is open for the orthodox Christian to say, in effect: "I cannot tell what has been the pilgrimage of Jesus Christ before his incarnation on this planet of ours, nor can I dare to prognosticate what his future role on other planets may be. I cannot see, however, why he should not be part of an evolutionary process too, although his stage in the process is infinitely beyond the one in which, by his grace, I am mercifully making some little progress here and now." So not even this objection need have the weight it seems to many Christians to carry.

Long before anyone knew of outer galaxies or could have thought seriously about the possibility of interplanetary travel, Alice Meynell (1847-1922), a profoundly mystical

English Catholic poet, hinted in a poem at the problem that
the magnitude of the universe posed for Christology even in
her time. Entitled *Christ in the Universe*, it contains allusions
such as these:

> No planet knows that this
> Our wayside planet, carrying land and wave,
> Love and life multiplied, and pain and bliss,
> Bears as chief treasure one forsaken grave.
>
> Nor, in our little day,
> May his devices with the heavens be guessed;
> His pilgrimage to thread the Milky Way,
> Or His bestowals there be manifest.
>
> But in the eternities
> Doubtless we shall compare together, hear
> A million alien gospels, in what guise
> He trod the Pleiades, the Lyre, the Bear.
>
> O, be prepared, my soul!
> To read the inconceivable, to scan
> The myriad forms of God those stars unroll
> When, in our turn we show to them a Man.[1]

The next objection to the reincarnational implicates of the
karmic law that I should like to consider here is partly
philosophical, partly theological. According to reincarnational teaching, the Self transcends in some way the personal-
ities into which it is periodically incarnated. We know,
however, that the brain functions as a computer and that this
computer not only deteriorates with age but can be irreparably
injured by an automobile accident or other traumatic experience in such a way as to destroy memory. The claims of
reincarnationists notwithstanding, it is plain that most
people remember nothing of a previous life and if what has

1. *The Golden Book of Modern English Poetry,* 1870-1920 (London and
Toronto: Dent and Sons, 1927), p. 51.

just been noticed about the functioning of the brain be true, that is unsurprising. For many Christians the notion of a "subtle body" or "etheric double" or "store of energy" to carry over from one incarnation to another the memory function seems fanciful, no less than does Plato's symbol of the waters of Lethe through which souls pass on their way to the next incarnation, so that all but a few indomitable and advanced souls who manage to keep their heads just a little above these waters of forgetfulness are completely deprived of the power to remember anything of an alleged past life.

This is, of course, a standard and serious philosophical objection (however answerable it may seem) to reincarnationism in general. We should notice, however, that what applies to the reincarnational goose applies no less to the Christian gander. Central to all Christian orthodoxy and the supreme focus of the *kerygma* or proclamation of the first apostles of Christianity is the doctrine of Resurrection. Because Jesus Christ has been "raised from the dead," those who acknowledge and receive him will rise too; that is, they will die but eventually receive a new body. Paul calls it a "glorious" body, one that is presumably finer and better, more ductile and of greater luminosity than our present one. But now, suppose that I have died and have been invested with this new and glorious body of which Paul so eloquently writes. Surely I must be filled with gratitude for what Christ did for me to make all this possible; yet how can I be able to have such thankfulness if I cannot remember my life in the physical body, the life in which my salvation was begun? And how can I remember anything about this life by means of my "glorified" brain or whatever instrument is its counterpart in the luminous body I have now been accorded? In short, whatever difficulties attend reincarnationist doctrine apply in exactly the same way to the indubitably orthodox Christian doctrine of the resurrection of the body.

Christians, especially those with a Catholic background, also often feel that the karmic principle and its reincarnational implicates encourage an individualist approach to such an extent as not only to remove the need for the Church, its

ministry, and its sacraments which the Church deems necessary for salvation, but also to eliminate all need of guidance
and help. True, reincarnationism, grounded in the karmic
principle, does make a "lone walk" possible. It does abolish
the need to depend absolutely on the Church's ministry and
sacraments. That is not to say, however, that any sane man or
woman, Christian or otherwise, would fail to use any help he
or she can find in so momentous an enterprise as one's salvation. After all, salvation is success in our spiritual evolution
where failure might have been. One uses and gives thanks for
whatever helps us to achieve it. The fact that I can, if I am
reasonably intelligent, educate myself entirely from books
does not imply that I shall on that account decline the services
of good teachers. On the contrary, the more intelligent I am
the more readily shall I see their value to me. Nevertheless,
in extremis I can do without a teacher and fend for myself. If it
should happen that I can find only very bad teachers, I may
well prefer to manage on my own, for a bad teacher may be
even worse than none. He or she may impede an intelligent
person's progress. So a stupid priest or ignorant rabbi or lazy
guru could be an impediment that I might well be better
without.

A thorough knowledge of the history of the Christian
Church leaves us in little doubt that much of the prejudice
against karmic and reincarnationist teaching has been
generated by the fears of those bad bishops and pedestrian
priests who, having no spirituality of their own to offer, perceive the danger that such spiritual independence poses to
their power over the lives of men and women. Good priests,
however, have nothing to fear and indeed everything to
welcome from the development of spiritual independence
among the faithful. In fact, many of the greatest Christians,
those who plainly have been conspicuously able to fend for
themselves in their spiritual development, have been no less
conspicuously ready to learn from any teacher or confessor or
friend and also to participate in the life of the Church with
the simplest of "babes" in the faith. One thinks, for instance, of
Teresa of Avila, of George Tyrrell, of Kierkegaard, of Simone

Weil, to mention only a random few. They have deeply loved the Church without finding it absolutely indispensable. I very much love my home without deeming it absolutely essential to life and happiness.

The suspicion, voiced long ago by A. E. Taylor in *The Faith of a Moralist*, that reincarnationism encourages procrastination also warrants notice. Of course one can put off reform to another life, but one knows all the while that one is only making things more difficult for oneself. Most people manage to procrastinate copiously even with no expectation of the "second chance" that reincarnationism provides. Augustine's youthful prayer "Give me chastity but not yet" is as possible without a karmic view as with one. The deathbed-repentance syndrome is familiar to all pastors and confessors. The moral urgency implied in either a reincarnationist or a nonreincarnationist view is always there. The sooner I reform, the easier my reformation will be; the longer I delay, the more trouble I make for myself. Every drunk learns that.

Some Christians object that reincarnationsim is inconsistent with the Christian teaching that our destiny is settled once for all at death. There is, however, no such clear Christian teaching. Indeed, the Christian teaching on the afterlife is, for various reasons, by far the most confused part of traditional theology. It is so for some very good reasons, one of which is that in the first century of the Christian Way people did not give it much thought because they expected the end of the world imminently, perhaps literally on the morrow. In such circumstances one does not readily engage in eschatological speculations. When eventually that expectation died down, churchmen were confronted with a vast panorama of possibilities from both their Hebrew heritage and their Hellenistic surroundings. The most promising line of early Christian thought was that which pointed to a state of purgation and growth, a notion which, found in Clement of Alexandria and others among the early Fathers, was later developed in singularly unfortunate ways in the Latin West as the medieval doctrine of purgatory. Along with this doctrine of an "intermediate state," however, were developed the notions of heaven and hell, states generally presented as unchanging conditions, the one of eternal bliss, the other of eternal torment. Such notions are in fact unthinkable not only because the doctrine of hell is incompatible with the doctrine of God's love and mercy, but because both heaven and hell exclude growth and evolution, which are of the very nature of all finite being. Most educated Christians have quietly set aside the notions of heaven and hell in the form in which they were presented in the Middle Ages and by the Reformation Fathers.

The objection that it is immoral to be held accountable for sins one has committed in a previous life and has therefore forgotten deserves some attention, since at first sight it seems plausible. How can I have the disposition of penitence for my misdeeds if I cannot even remember them? We may well argue that if a child is to be punished the punishment should be swift, since otherwise the child will soon have forgotten the wrong he or she did and therefore rightly resent the punishment. But while that may be sound parental practice for the training of the very young, life operates on different lines. Modern psychoanalysis recognizes that what gives us most trouble is what lies buried in our unconscious. It is our forgotten misdeeds and evil thoughts that take the worst toll. Christian theology abundantly recognizes the fact that we do not know how distorted we are. Like it or not, we do have to pay the price for past wrongdoing we have forgotten about. It is so easy to injure my brother and then forget about it. The greater the injury the more ready I am to forget, that is, to push the memory of it down into my unconscious. There, however, it continues to fester. The reincarnationist, grounded as he is in the karmic principle, is only extending the scene, knowing as he does that man has a much longer history than the date on his birth certificate. He has also a longer future than the date that is to be on his death certificate: a future he can make or mar.

Many Christians believe in a literalistic way in the Second Coming of Christ as a "day," the *dies irae*, the Day of Judgment. Is not that alien to a reincarnationist view? It may be incompatible with some forms of reincarnationism, but not all. We can still interpret the Day of Judgment as the end of the present age and the beginning of a new one, which is indeed in accord with the biblical witness. The new age, if this planet Earth be destroyed, might begin on another planet in another galaxy, if not on one in our own. The holocaust that many Christians envision on that "terrible day" would presumably in any case wipe out all life, including the vast animal kingdom to which we are biologically related through evolution.

The Cambridge moralist, A. C. Ewing, in a sympathetic but critical reference to reincarnationism and the karmic principle, suggested that it has too much of a "mercantile flavor," too much of "an exact proportion between such incommensurables as goodness and happiness." In such a scenario, he suggests, there could be no genuine self-sacrifice. True, Christian love knows nothing of moral accountancy. Christ, far from calculating the cost of our redemption, pours forth his blood for us on the Cross with infinite abandon. The cost of our redemption, however, may be even greater than Ewing perceived. Thomas Aquinas, pre-eminent among the medieval schoolmen, taught that grace presupposes nature and perfects it. If then, God, in his self-humbling, must reckon with both law and nature, the cost of sacrificial love must surely be incalculably higher than we can imagine. The karmic principle abides.

Perhaps, however, nothing so much impedes the christening of karma as does the notion that emphasizing individual responsibility for salvation undercuts the operation of Christ's redemptive act. Since this is probably the most popular misconception on the subject, especially among Protestant Christians, I wish to make abundantly clear to readers, Christian or otherwise, that this objection arises more from a misunderstanding of Christian doctrine than from a misunderstanding of the karmic principle itself. The notion, prevalent in certain circles, that the recipient of grace, being assured of salvation, may then sit back at ease is, of course, accounted notably heretical. It is a form of what theologians call "antinomianism": the notion that the Gospel puts one above or beyond the law. That is a pernicious travesty of

Christian doctrine as taught in the New Testament, the early Fathers, and not least the Reformation Fathers. A tradition that runs all the way from Paul through Augustine to Luther and Calvin demands that Christians be especially on their guard against the notion that when one 'has become aware of the saving act of Christ in the soul there is nothing more to be done.

In another book of mine, I have told the story of a stuttering Christian missionary who, on being taunted that Christ did not seem to have healed him, replied: "But b-b-before he h-h-healed me I was a d-d-deaf-m-m-mute." Until his conversion his condition had been hopeless; now it was remediable. There is also an old Victorian poem about a little girl who, having covered her school "slate" with figures in trying to solve an arithmetic problem, comes weeping to the teacher who, being a good and kind teacher, sits down beside the child, cleans the slate and says, "Now let us do it together." The teacher's action becomes, in the poem, a parable of the work of salvation that Christ begins in the soul. Would such an action diminish the gratitude of such a child? Should such a recognition of the nature of Christ's saving love diminish a Christian's appreciation and gratitude? Of course not. If you had a mental block against mathematics that made math a fruitless pain to you, its removal would make doing math a pleasure; the last thing it would do for you would be to cause you to stop doing mathematics. If you were an alcoholic down and out in the gutter and then through Christ found your way to redemption from your vice and the path to a productive and creative life, the last thing you would do would be to insist that you had no longer any need to consider the tendency that had brought you so low in the first place. On the contrary, you would be all the more aware of it and at the same time aware of your power to overcome it, which you did not have before.

"So then, my dear friends," writes Paul to the Church at Philippi, "continue to do as I tell you, as you always have; not only as you did when I was there with you, but even more now that I am no longer there; and work for your salvation 'in fear and trembling.' It is God, for his own loving purposes, who puts both the will and the action into you." (Philippians 2.12f. Jerusalem Bible)

Is there, then, any sound theological reason from any Christian point of view, orthodox or heterodox, traditionalist or experimental, against the christening of karma and its reincarnational implicates? Personally I cannot see any at all. The influence on Christianity of Hellenistic ideas, including of course the Platonic tradition, was not merely something that developed after the apostles of the Christian Way had spread their message to the Gentile world; it was present, to say the least, in the Judaism in which the Christian Way was cradled. During what Christian scholars have customarily called the "intertestamental period" (that is, approximately 165 B.C.E. through A.D. 48, the interval between the last book of the Hebrew canon, Daniel, and the earliest of the New Testament writings), the Jews were exposed to vast extraneous influences. Jewish thought, even in Palestine, was profoundly affected by these. The kind of movement of which Jesus was the center, however we may choose to interpret it, would have been unthinkable in Palestine a few centuries earlier. By his time, however, the situation had so altered that Hellenistic ideas could be commingled with traditional Jewish faith and practice in a rabbi's teaching. In Alexandria, the chief intellectual center of the Diaspora, the Hellenistic influence was overwhelming, having a most able spokesman in Philo, a contemporary of Jesus; but even in the Jewish Homeland its effects, if less enduring, were considerable. Greek architectural ideas affected even the way in which synagogues were built and Greek administrative practices were adopted by Jewish communities in their government and organization. Hellenism was fostered, at least for a time, by the priestly aristocracy. While Jesus himself encouraged the veneration of the Torah and in principle honored the traditional Jewish ritual and other customs, his leadership of the kind of celibate religious community into which he organized his disciples was alien to classical Hebrew practice. The *extent* to which Hellenistic ideas affected his teaching is controversial; what is indisputable is that Hellenistic ideas had so permeated the thought of his time that (as we know from Qumran and other sources) the kind of ministry in which he engaged and the sort of community he gathered around him were part of the scenario of the day. Few could have been ignorant of their existence. To suggest otherwise would be like suggesting that an educated American today could be ignorant of Darwin or of Freud or that he or she might not have heard of nuclear fission.

We all know that Plato, following the Pythagorean tradition, accepted the ancient doctrine of reincarnation, very explicitly putting it into the mouth of the Socrates of the Dialogues. Long before Christianity was in the way of being directly influenced by Platonistic and Neoplatonistic ideas in the pagan world, however, it had emerged in an atmosphere in which reincarnationist ideas such as Plato took as part of the ideological scenery were at least an ingredient. Christians of the first century could not but have imbibed such ideas and there is some evidence to show that they did not by any means necessarily repudiate them. Some seem to have found them congenial. In the Alexandrian tradition that developed, in which Clement and Origen played leading roles, the thought of Plato loomed very large indeed.

Why, then, did reincarnationist teaching get such a bad press in the Christian Church and come to be so much distrusted, not to say feared? Only a combination of circumstances that included the inchoate state of Christian eschatology and the second-century Church leaders' suspicion of Gnostic teaching, could have led to the ousting of a reincarnationist interpretation of the life of the world to come that was and is the Christian hope. I think this result has gravely impoverished the Church's official presentation of the nature of the afterlife. As we have seen, there is really not the slightest reason for the fear or the distrust.

Of course that is not to say that reincarnationism in every form in which it happens to appear is necessarily reconcilable with Christian faith or that the Church ought to welcome Gnosticism no matter in what guise it comes. In some forms it can lead to and indeed express a selfish unconcern for others that would be radically antithetical to the *agapé* that Paul exalts above all else in one of his most eloquent passages (I Corinthians 13) and that is universally acclaimed by Christians as of the very life of the Church. Any *such* reincarnationism would be, on that account alone, entirely out of court. Moreover, reincarnationist teaching is sometimes so closely tied to certain metaphysical presuppositions not easily if at all reconcilable to Christian faith that a Christian with any pretensions to loyalty to the central creeds of the Church would be rightly cautious in regard to such forms of it. Nevertheless, when all that is said, there is nothing in the notion itself and certainly nothing in the karmic principle that lies behind it (whatever name be given to that principle) that need give a Christian of even the strictest orthodox stance the slightest pause. On the contrary, the karmic principle and its reincarnationist implicates can be warmly embraced by any such Christian as a means of greatly illuminating his or her understanding of the nature of the life of the world to come, belief in which is solemnly affirmed in the final article of the Nicene Creed with no specifying or limiting details of any kind. Cardinal Mercier is among the distinguished Roman Catholics who have declared that reincarnationism has never really been officially or explicitly condemned by the Church. The bad press it received was partly through a sort of guilt by association with other ideas and partly because of the fears we have considered earlier.[2]

2. This chapter is reproduced (with some modification) by kind permission of the Theosophical Publishing House from my article "The Christening of Karma" in V. Hanson and R. Stewart (eds.), *Karma* (Wheaton, IL: Theosophical Publishing House, 1981).

6

Karma and Freedom

Who then is free? The wise man alone, who is a stern master to himself, whom neither poverty nor death nor bonds affright, who has the courage to say "no" again and again to desires, to despise the objects of ambition, who is a whole in himself, smoothed and rounded.

Horace, *Satires*

Where justice reigns, 'tis freedom to obey.

James Montgomery, *Greenland*

We have seen that the karmic principle entails a recognition of freedom of choice. Although karma may restrict freedom of choice by imposing limiting conditions, the karmic principle, far from implying a fatalism or determinism, is fundamentally a "freewill" principle.

The concept of freedom is a notoriously thorny one in the history of serious philosophic thought. Modern linguistic analysis draws attention to certain difficulties to which we must give some attention in the present chapter. We should note first of all, however, that the old mechanistic, Newtonian physics was inhospitable to the notion of freedom of choice, because it seemed irreconcilable with the "laws" of physics as then understood. Indeed, despite the indeterminacy that Heisenberg and others have perceived in the cosmic structure, the belief generally still prevails, even in intellectual circles, that human consciousness itself is a puzzle, having no place in the scientific understanding of the universe and the "laws of nature" governing it. On this widespread view, the gulf between the "natural" sciences and the humanities seems unbridgeable. Without such a bridge, the prospect of reconciling the moral aspect of evolution to the biological one is indeed dim. Since the karmic principle is unintelligible apart from a recognition of the possibility of freedom of choice, the questions to be treated in the present chapter are of crucial importance for the subject of this book.

Why should we trouble with the old Newtonian physics, now outmoded by quantum theory with all its immense consequences for the reconciliation of the karmic principle to scientific thought? Simply because the presuppositions of the old, Newtonian view die hard, being still found even among intelligent and educated people, including even some contemporary philosophers, who, although of course they know about quantum theory, have not adequately taken its consequences into account.

The old physics could find no place for human consciousness and the phenomena relating to it because its presuppositions were thoroughly deterministic. The properties it recognized were mere aggregates of certain properties that could be enumerated like the elements in chemistry. Consciousness was not on the list, and since it behaved very differently from anything that was listed, it was plainly not eligible for inclusion. No means could be found to make it fit. Moreover and even more importantly, the old physics was already complete without the concept of consciousness, so it could be excluded as a gratuitous addition to an already complete system and therefore it could be left to philosophers and theologians to make what they could of it on their own. It was their plaything; they could talk about it as they talked about intelligence and freedom, about imagination and reflection; but such enterprises could not expect the blessing of the scientific academies, which neither needed them nor could accommodate them.

Quantum physics, by contrast, claims no *such* completeness. In quantum theory is an incompleteness, an indeterminateness, that suggests, at least, a place for freedom of choice. Such is the nature of quantum physics that new choices continue to have to be made and they are made, indeed, when human beings appear on the scene. A new dimension of reality has emerged that demands new choices.

Moreover, if we consider what neurophysiologists can tell us of the neural structure of the human brain, we can see that human freedom may be identified with a specific part of the general freedom that quantum theory provides. The conscious event in the brain can be identified with a functionally equivalent physical event. So a connection between the "natural" sciences and the humanities can be established on the basis of the identity of the event of consciousness with the functionally equivalent physical event.

All this gives rise to a new way of asking epistemological questions. We all know, of course, that our perceptual world is constructed from selective information from our environment. How, for instance, might our world look if we could see X-rays? Our ordinary color experience is the result of an internal functioning of properties of our brain. The evolutionary development of the brain, then, has a function in the development of the way we experience our environment. Of course if we are free to open ourselves to new experiences, we are also free to close ourselves off from them. Narrowmindedness and unimaginativeness are eminently possible and notoriously too often prevail. At every step in the selective process, however, we are confronted with the possibility of choice, and such is the richness and complexity of our environment, physical and mental, that we must select and group our experiences, whatever be the principle on which we make the selecting and grouping. Human freedom of choice becomes, then, not only a reality but the reality that makes possible our fuller perception of the nature of the universe and of its grandeur, its richness, and its multidimensionality. In the making of choices we can participate more fully in the reality around us and attune ourselves to it and can even come to perceive the principle of human freedom itself, which is in the karmic law.

Nevertheless, we ought to recognize that no satisfactory scientific explanation has been provided for consciousness in man and other organisms. Neurophysiologists have not succeeded in explaining, for example, mental imagery and thought processes, let alone volition, in a way that would provide an adequate account of what that imagery and those processes mean in terms of the spiritual awareness that we do in fact possess. Through evolution, the nervous system of mammals has been raised to the point that eventually has made human consciousness possible. Some primitive form of consciousness, however, may be found in even the most rudimentary forms of life. Even amoebae apparently have some primitive form of awareness of food particles and other objects, crude though it be compared with ours. We cannot easily account, however, for the fact (if it be a fact) that I can and do choose to resist engaging in a course of action that is exceedingly pleasurable in favor of one that is distinctly painful because the latter seems to me conducive to what I take to be a nobler end or higher goal. Of course some psychoanalysts and others have deterministic theories about this; but such theories, with the presuppositions underlying them, still more plainly fail to provide a satisfactory explanation of our awareness of the reality of making choices.

Then is the freedom that I believe I possess a mere delusion, or is my claim to it authentic? We get much encouragement from modern quantum physics for repudiating the "hard determinist" views that some thinkers are still willing to accept; yet quantum theory does not provide us with any means of actually justifying a belief in what is traditionally called freedom of choice. Presumably it should not be expected to do so. The question is crucial for those who hope to entertain the recognition of any principle such as the karmic one, which is meaningless unless we can establish in some way the authenticity of the claim of spiritually minded people to make genuine decisions freely, notwithstanding the limitations on that freedom imposed by the obstacles that impede them and the burdens which, like Sinbad's, oppress them.

First we must try to define freedom of choice. When we talk of free choice, what precisely is to be understood by the adjective "free"? Strictly, it adds nothing to the noun "choice," being a value-word such as *healthy* or *unobstructed*. A healthy body is a body that functions as a body should; a free flow of blood in the arteries is one that is not impeded by anything such as a clot. So to say of choice that it is free can be only to say that, being unobstructed in its course by any external agency, it is able to function freely as choices should function. But how should choices function? When we examine the word "free" more closely, we find that it is sometimes descriptive, sometimes evaluative. When at the airport the traffic controllers signal the pilot that all is clear for his takeoff, they are telling him that there is nothing in his way. The plane may then fly freely in the way that we think planes ought to fly. Yet if the message were in error and the plane collided with another, could we say that the plane did not fly the way planes ought to fly? On the contrary, it flew freely, as did the other plane, but unfortunately neither flew the way we *like* planes to fly, for the collision would have been a tragic disaster for many families.

Planes have, of course, no capacity for the kind of freedom of choice that is being claimed for human beings. When, however, we examine a human claim to freedom, we find that it is evaluative and is therefore disputable, since our judgment on it will depend on our understanding of the nature of the good. A single man may say he is free, being relieved of the burden of the care of a family; but a happily married man may question the value the bachelor attaches to his celibate state. A sannyâsi or mendicant friar may claim he is free, being relieved of the cares of the world and of attachment to a complex and corrupt society; but the successful businessman who sees the emaciated features and calloused feet of the religious beggar may see in him nothing but a hobo burdened with poverty, loneliness, and hunger, from which the businessman feels free.

If, however, we think of freedom in abstraction from the purposes to which it is put, we begin to see more clearly what it is that protagonists of the claim to freedom of choice are affirming. When we say that a healthy body is a better state of affairs than an unhealthy one, we are making the value

judgment that it is best *in principle* for a body to be unobstructed in its functioning by anything that would inhibit its
functioning as a body should function. The owner of the
body we call healthy may use it in ways we do not at all ap-
prove (he might commit murder, for instance); yet, much as
we deplore such a use of a healthy body, we cannot but recognize that, even if I be harboring such murky intentions, it is
better *in principle* that I should be unimpeded in my ability to
think and speak and act, no matter what my thoughts and
words and actions may turn out to be. So I account freedom a
primary value as I account health a primary value. My health
is not a value to the invading bacteria that my healthy body
readily destroys; but since I am not a bacterium but the
beneficiary of a healthy human body, I do not concern myself
with points of view (if they may be so called) so far from
human interests, for I deem the latter much more important.

Recognition of the karmic principle always presupposes
that I am better off with the ability to make choices unimpeded, if only because I am then at least theoretically able to
choose to act according to the order and harmony that are at
the heart of all things. Unfortunately, however, I am in fact
demonstrably impeded in many ways from the exercise of
that freedom of choice. For instance, while the choice I wish
to make may be to show patience in a trying situation or
toward a troublesome person, my will to do so is impeded by
my short temper: a circumstance that could be as obstructive
to my volitional capacity as would be a fractured arm to a
person who sought to lift a blind child out of danger. The
fact that my quick temper may be my own fault or due to my
own karma from the past does not affect the result any more
than does the drunk driver's fault affect the outcome of his
drunk driving.

No human freedom is infinite. My freedom is always circumscribed in one way or another, if only by the date and
place of my birth, my heredity, my social condition, my
physical health, and my mental capacity. These all limit my
exercise of freedom as much as my physical limitations as a
human animal limit the height I can jump with even the most

rigorous training and the most unusual physical endowment.

Yet surely nothing is more remarkable in human life than the fact that those with the most restrictive circumstances often have the most remarkable accomplishments to their credit. No doubt many others have felt the embarrassment I have personally experienced in finding a blind man able to solve a mechanical problem faster than I could and no less quickly give effect to its solution. Those of us with a notable strike against us in life (be it poverty or ill health or a loveless home or whatever) do not fare better than others by luck but, rather, by a better use of what we have, little though it seem to be as we engage in the struggle. Being disadvantaged, we try harder.

What is distinctive about the concept of karma is that those who recognize it as the basic "law" of all being are affirming that even the circumstances that impede the exercise of my freedom, standing as obstacles to be overcome, are in themselves in one way or another self-induced. Not only are my failings such as short temper or avarice or sloth self-induced, as would be widely admitted; so also are even my congenital circumstances: I chose even my parents. Yet when I chose them my choice was already circumscribed by the choices I had made before. I certainly could not choose them as easily as I might choose an overcoat from a rack in a department store, because I had already a burden of karma that limited the freedom I could exercise. Karma is a two-edged sword: it entails that freedom of choice that has resulted in my self-made obstructions as surely as it preserves the limited freedom that I enjoy. That freedom is my priceless instrument in making it possible for me to extricate myself from the effects of the bad karma I have laid up and clear the way to greater and greater freedom. My bad habits do not merely impede me as does a stalled car or other obstacle that gets in my way as I am trying to pass; they bind me as surely as do a prisoner's handcuffs or leg irons, restricting my movements in such a way that it can never be merely a question of kicking an unwelcome obstacle out of my way but rather of extricating myself from the shackles of my own making.

The truth of all this must surely be evident to anyone who understands even minimally the state of his or her psyche. What karmic doctrine does is to extend the psychoanalyst's scenario to my entire history, my history before as well as during my present life. Karma can be considered either in terms of obstacles or the absence of obstacles, the removal of which gives my will freedom to act, affording me a genuine choice. Take a pedestrian sort of example: when I have no money I cannot choose to buy anything; when I have a hundred dollars I am free to choose among several possibilities. Paradoxical though it may seem, however, the fact that I have a million dollars to spend may incline me to spend more recklessly and therefore inhibit my freedom of choice more than I would be inhibited by having only a hundred dollars to spend. Those with the highest endowments, mental, spiritual, or physical, do not by any means always use them to the best advantage. Those whose endowments are most meager often do so in an astonishing degree. The race is not always to the swift, nor is the battle always to the strong. What matters is how we use what we have. Such is the freedom that the karmic principle provides for us that we *can* make karmic limitations work for us better than karmic endowments.

Paradoxes relating to freedom of choice abound. We find one, for instance, in the exergue to this chapter: "where justice reigns, 'tis freedom to obey." Obedience seems at first sight the antithesis of personal freedom. Is not release from the yoke of obedience to a master a prerequisite for the attainment of freedom? Obedience to society's capricious rules may be in many ways as inhibiting to my personal freedom as would be a state of serfdom; but if the society's rules were really perfectly just, then obedience to them could be indeed a greater exercise of freedom than I could otherwise make. As following the dictates of my healthy body keeps it functioning well, so obedience to the moral law affords me greater freedom than could any attempt to resist it.

We must also distinguish between the enjoyment of freedom (a theoretical advantage) and its exercise (a practical act). When we are unaware of constraints, we are unaware of freedom, yet we unwittingly exercise it, as was the case with Adam and Eve in the Garden of Eden story. When we are aware of constraints, we struggle to exercise our freedom as a drowning man struggles to survive or a choking man to regain his breath. Most ambulatory persons are generally unimpressed by the fact that they are free to walk, for it seldom if ever occurs to them that the situation might be otherwise. Anyone who has been paralyzed and is recovering gradually from the paralysis is likely, by contrast, to be overjoyed by the discovery of even a modest remnant of his old capacity for walking. Wishing beyond all else to regain his walking power, he chooses (within the very narrow path of action still open to him) to make a Herculean effort to attain a goal that in his ambulatory days was so easily attainable as to be not seen as a goal at all. It is in such extreme cases that we can begin to see what the protagonists of a freewill doctrine are defending.

The determinist case, however, is not to be lightly dismissed, least of all by those who see the karmic principle at the heart of all things. For of course the karmic principle has a deterministic aspect too, in the sense that there are certainly obvious limits on human freedom. For each one of us, the path of our life is mapped out for us by a variety of circumstances that are handed to us at birth. The general geography of that path and the obstacles attending it are given as surely as is a hand at bridge. If we try to ignore them, we shall only hit our heads upon them. We can circumvent them, however, or otherwise reach the end of the road despite the troublesome impediments to our doing so, and it is in this scenario that my action, the exercise of my will to act, can be seen in its true light. Action can never be understood except in the act of performing it any more than can feeling be understood except in the feeling of whatever it is that is felt. Action, in the strictest sense of the word, always entails a liberation of oneself from some inhibiting circumstance.

So then we may say: karma deals us the hand; we choose how to play it. If the hand is a poor one the reason lies in how we have lived before; it is our inheritance, like an ancestral title to land. Yet our spiritual success in this life lies in what we do with what we get. As we have seen, you may do better with a poor hand than I do with a good one. That is what matters. Spiritual freedom does not come in units like so many shares of stock or so many bond coupons. We create it within the confines of our karma. That is why the karmic principle, despite the deterministic element in it, is so radically a free-will principle. Hence the importance and relevance of what we have been considering in this chapter.

7

Evolution, Karma, and Rebirth

*Like the doctrine of evolution itself, that of transmigration
has its roots in the world of reality.*
Thomas Huxley, *Evolution and Ethics*

Throughout the course of our study so far we have dealt with
reincarnation as an implicate of the karmic principle. Rightly
so, in the sense that these two doctrines have been traditionally
treated together as two sides of the same coin. Such is the
karmic "law" that it could not be worked out on a scale so
narrow as that of one little human life. Such is the doctrine
of reincarnation that without the karmic principle it would
be at best a mere description of the capricious behavior of
the gods of a primitive folklore. It is only in combination that
the two doctrines make sense, morally and intellectually.

When we go on, however, to see reincarnation not only in
the light of karma but in conjunction with the evolutionary
principle, the connection cannot be so easily taken for granted,
even by those accustomed to think in karmic and reincarnational terms. For evolutionism, as it has been developed in
modern thought under the impetus of Darwin's biological studies, cannot be said to be historically inseparable
from the other two. At any rate, it raises questions about
reincarnation that require the attention that is now to

95

be given them in the present chapter.

Nevertheless, one does not have to go far in reflecting upon the implicates of a spiritual interpretation of evolution to see that reincarnationist hypotheses lie round the corner. The question is, rather, what kind of reincarnationism best fits an evolutionary understanding both of the cosmos and of man?

We all know that character and personality traits reappear from one generation to another and that these can be understood genetically. This would be indeed obvious even without any scientific investigations at all, for it can be seen in almost any family. When evolution is seen in the light of an understanding of the "law" of karma, however, it leads us to question whether such "genetic rebirth" is the only kind of reincarnation. It shows us what was well known to the teachers of the Ancient Wisdom: reincarnation is much more than that, although that may have a part to play in the process.

In other works of mine[1] I have called attention to the fact that the weakest and most confused part of Christian theology is its doctrine of the future life. That this is so is due to a variety of circumstances in the complex situation prevailing in the Mediterranean world at the time of Christian beginnings. Nevertheless, the absence of any definite understanding of an evolutionary principle in the universe aggravated all of them. The Bible itself provided a heritage of very conflicting views on the subject of the hereafter. The Hebrews in primitive times had had vague suppositions about what happened in Sheol, the underground abode of the dead: a shadowy place conceived somewhat as Homer imagined Hades. Under the influence of foreign ideas, however, after their exile, they entertained a variety of opinions. The Pharisees, for example, held some form of a doctrine of resurrection. Then in the first century of the Christian era and to some extent even later the expectation among Christians that Christ would return soon (that is, any day) prevailed so generally that speculation about the nature of the hereafter was discouraged. No doubt

1. For example, my *Reincarnation in Christianity* (Wheaton, Il.: Theosophical Publishing House, 1978).

they felt they would know soon enough, so that it was idle to inquire. Until the Copernican revolution, moreover, a geocentric cosmology induced a narrow, parochial view of our place in the universe. In Protestantism, furthermore, the absence of any doctrine of an intermediate state such as purgatory (which, I contend, may be reincarnationally interpreted) accentuated the tendency to think of human life as a unique sojourn in time, hedged on either side by eternity.

Such an attitude toward human life had strange consequences for the Western mind, affecting both believers and unbelievers. For the notion that one makes a sudden entry into existence at birth and is then at death no less suddenly plunged into an eternity of salvation or damnation could not but color the concept of God that generally prevailed in the West. At worst it made God seem an arbitrary tyrant who handed out notably unequal chances to people yet judged them in the end as if each had been endowed alike. At best it made God seem mysteriously and unaccountably benevolent to a few whom he arbitrarily selected for redemption. To believer and unbeliever alike it obscured the gracious and loving nature of divine Being while paying lip service to the notion of a God of love who could not but look very much the opposite, his capricious excursions into benevolence notwithstanding. True, it did tend to induce in many a sense of urgency about moral decision, but at the price of unnecessary mystification about the role of this life in human destiny and therefore about the nature of the God who was hailed as controlling it.

The concept of evolution, while it does not necessarily entail a reincarnationist view of life, makes such a view eminently plausible, however reincarnation may be interpreted. It certainly makes singularly implausible the traditionally confused accounts of human destiny with which the official pronouncements of the Church have saddled the West. Reincarnationism comes in several forms and an evolutionary understanding of the universe makes all of them worthy of serious consideration. Nevertheless, the one that has come down to us in Indian thought and that has played a greater role in the West (if through underground channels) than many suppose, should certainly deserve close scrutiny, to say the least, by all who have perceived the crucial importance of evolution in modern thought.

The theme of reincarnation had a prominent role in Greek philosophy, which is the source and cradle of the intellectual traditions of Europe and America. Plato makes his Socrates talk of the transmigration of souls not only as though it were part of the basic intellectual furniture of his day but as the personal belief of one who preferred to die by drinking the appointed draught of hemlock rather than accept what he took to be an ignominious compromise that would have saved his life in face of the appallingly unjust sentence of an Athenian court. Plato accepts the doctrine of the transmigration of souls as part of his intellectual scenario, and it has played a role, overtly or covertly, in our Western heritage of thought ever since.

Only in the last century, however, has it been possible for us to consider in any very useful way the connection between evolution and rebirth. For only when thinking people had considered the implications of biological evolution as it was presented by Darwin and Huxley could they go on to perceive the implications for the concept of a spiritual, interior evolution such as ethical forms of reincarnation entail. On such reincarnationist views, our spirituality is not a mere outgrowth or by-product of biological development but arises, instead, from the creative principle in all things. The view that the body develops and exudes the soul somewhat as the liver secretes bile (traditionally called epiphenomenalism) is expressly repudiated by Plato's Socrates in his conversation with Simmias, who upholds an ancient form of that view.

Although seeds of evolutionary ideas are to be found in the ancient forms of thought that are our Western heritage, the mental mold of the Middle Ages was (on the whole and despite exceptions) inhospitable to ideas of this kind. With the Italian Renaissance, however, they began to be in various ways adumbrated. Notable among thinkers who expounded evolutionary ideas is Giordano Bruno (1548-1600), the last seven years of whose life were spent in imprisonment for heresy in the notorious Castel Sant' Angelo, Rome, and who was eventually burned at the stake on the Campo dei Fiori on February 17, 1600. Bruno explicitly proposed an evolutionary philosophy in the form of a progressive development of nature, thereby anticipating in his own way the conclusions of Darwin, although lacking, of course, the extensive evidence Darwin was able to adduce for his own conclusions.

Bruno's best known and probably his most provocative work was his *Spacio de la Bestia Trionfante*, published in 1584. It is an allegory in which he praises philosophy and denigrates popular religion. Both Spinoza and Leibniz were influenced by aspects of Bruno's teaching. Bruno unambiguously favors a reincarnationist doctrine as at least likely. He suggests that the reason we have no clear recollection of previous lives is that our souls, unburdened by such recollections, will prize their present life more and therefore concentrate on living it to the full without any undue dreaming about past or future lives.[2]

Like Aristotle, Bruno held that there is nothing in the intellect that is not first in the senses. Unlike Aristotle, who saw the infinite as the irrational (as did the Christian schoolmen who followed him), Bruno saw it as laying the ground for an understanding of the perfection of the infinitude of the physical universe. Bruno may have been less disciplined than some thinkers; yet neither is he as uncritical as some of his critics would have us suppose. He could not allow that one method, be it empiricist or rationalist, or one view, monistic or pluralistic, could by itself provide the sole means of attaining truth or be in itself the only correct way of presenting it. Perhaps because of this openminded attitude, Bruno was probably the first thinker after the Middle Ages to work out an evolutionary theory about the universal movement of matter and the transformation of lower into higher organisms and to treat the human mind as a special factor in the evolution of the human race.

2. G. Bruno, *The Expulsion of the Triumphant Beast*, tr. A. D. Imerti (New Brunswick, N.J.: Rutgers University Press, 1964), pp. 94-95.

Bruno is prominent among Renaissance thinkers who perceived, however dimly, a connection between evolution and rebirth. As we have seen, however, it was only after Darwin that thinkers in the Anglo-Saxon world could have developed the theological interpretations of evolutionism that they did, along definitely Christian lines and long before Teilhard de Chardin. Despite the erudition that he acknowledged in the thinkers of the English-speaking world, they seemed to him far too narrowly tied to a positivistic sort of empiricism. Yet Sir Julian Huxley, who first met Teilhard in Paris in 1946, had already in some ways adumbrated Teilhard's thesis, at least to the extent of envisioning human evolution and biological evolution as two phases of a single process: a thesis Sir Julian later developed in his *Uniqueness of Man*. Teilhard's occasional disparagement of the Anglo-Saxon tendency, common among continental European philosophers, is often justified; but if Teilhard had known more of the work of the late nineteenth-century American interpreters of the creative process, he would surely have paid tribute to them. Be all that as it may, neither Teilhard nor his American Protestant forerunners connected evolutionism with rebirth in any significant way. The theological climate that both Protestant and Catholic thinkers had to face in those days, even in "advanced" circles, was such that a Christian evolutionism was for both a sufficiently novel, not to say startling, proposal in itself, without compounding it with reincarnationism.

Still, although these late nineteenth- and early twentieth-century thinkers could not have gone explicitly further than they did without alienating the very audiences that they in fact so powerfully influenced, their evolutionary stance was not without roots in the history of ideas. Moreover, their aim of reconciling the religion of their day with the science of their day had been indeed the motivation behind the work of Thomas Aquinas in the thirteenth century. Thomas, in his opposition to the "double-truth" theory of the Latin Averroists, who taught that there are two different kinds of truth, insisted that truth must be one. Therefore the religious truths found in the Bible cannot conflict with (although they may go beyond) any philosophical or scientific truth that can be independently shown. Recognition of the significance of the evolutionary principle in nature is to be found in German thinkers nearer the age of the great nineteenth-century controversies about such questions: in Friedrich Wilhelm Schelling (1775-1854), for instance, who died five years before the publication of *The Origin of Species* and was the leading disciple of Friedrich Christoph Oetinger (1702-82).

Oetinger was in turn in the tradition of Jakob Boehme (1575-1624). Boehme, an important figure in the history of theosophical Christian mysticism, influenced the thought of Hegel and others in Germany and that of the Christian Platonists and others in England. Isaac Newton was among those who diligently read him. Boehme, although untutored in any conventional sense (he was at first a shepherd, then for many years a cobbler) was a man of extraordinary insight, who saw the spiritual significance of nature and taught his disciples to see the spiritual significance of the sciences that study nature. Oetinger saw redemption as cosmic and the whole universe as included in a process of transfiguration by Christ. On his view the physical world is the corporeal manifestation of the splendor of divine Being.

Franz Xaver von Baader (1765-1841), a theologian who also read Boehme, used evolution as a category both of the history of nature and of the history of salvation. However, only where theosophical insights of one sort or another have prevailed has the intimate connection between evolution and rebirth been clearly perceived. Not unexpectedly it is found in the writers of the theosophical renaissance in England and America in the late nineteenth century, for the idea of evolution was then in the air, not only because of the work of Darwin but also as a result of the evolutionist thought then developing in the world of humane letters.

From our perspective today we can see that biological evolution on our planet seems to be no longer producing any radically new species of life. Nor is man undergoing any noteworthy biological change, such as growing wings or fins.

Indeed, nothing seems to be further from the case. Yet although biological evolution has apparently stopped, a new "invisible" human evolution has been for long taking place and is now in process at an accelerated speed. Conspicuous in this interior evolutionary process is the immense advance in the attainment of human freedom that is discernible in some individuals. Humanity has become *capable* as never before of guiding its interior evolutionary process and therefore the destiny of the human race as such.

The freedom of humanity to guide its evolution is not infinite; no freedom is. Nevertheless, it is of crucial significance. With the power that humanity is so dramatically developing in the social dimension, with all its attendant moral responsibilities, comes inevitably greater spiritual freedom, and also new responsibilities, in the individual. The individual, in confronting the evolutionary struggles of humanity and adjusting to them, whets his or her personal capacity on the grinding stone of the society to which he or she belongs. One gradually takes over the evolutionary drive of humanity, acquiring more and more the capacity to choose for oneself. No longer does one merely whirl with the evolutionary spiral; one learns how to take off on one's own. As Emerson long ago observed, no bird soars too high if he soars on his own wings. Yet this sense of independence of humanity as such brings an immensely enhanced sense of one's interdependence with the realm of the spirit, under whatever guise the spirit may come. So my humanness becomes the catalyst for my individuality. Immortality does not reside in humanity as such; it is I who may attain it through using my human pilgrimage to transcend my humanity.

If, then, the function of humanity is to minister to the interior, spiritual evolutionary process, to spin off individuals who are en route for a still higher destiny, then humanity itself becomes no less than but also no more than the mother of the individuals who attain their spiritual freedom through her. Humanity becomes for the individual in his struggle for spiritual evolution what Mother Church is, in her own fashion, for those who follow the Christian Way. As mother, humanity nourishes, sustains, conserves and stabilizes the process but does not initiate it or develop it, for only the individual can do that. By the same token, wise human beings will instinctively shrink from any course of action (ecological shortsightedness and certain nuclear projects are obvious examples) that might endanger the survival of the human race as such. For if humanity is my mother I will see (as a child instinctively sees) that what endangers my mother endangers me and can impede the development of my capacity for freedom.

But how, then, on such a model, is the individual to acquire this freedom we are talking about? Jesus tells his disciples: "you will learn the truth and the truth shall make you free" (John 8.32). Yet such learning is not to be accomplished overnight. Not even in one little lifetime can such freedom be won. Even the longest and most remarkable of human lives could not by itself provide the means of attaining it. Theoretically, perhaps yes; practically, no. As well might one expect the ocean tides to wear great rocks by the sea-shore into sand in a few months. If we are to take seriously the notion of a genuine spiritual evolution in the individual after biological evolution on our planet has virtually ceased, the individual must have time to achieve it. Since it has taken billions of years to bring into existence our primeval human ancestors, I can hardly expect to transcend my human state in one lifetime. That marvellous process has taken time, is taking time, and will take more time.

That spiritual evolution should take place at all, no matter in how long a time, should be wonder enough. Christians, in acknowledging their debt to Christ in making the process possible for them, would be churlish in supposing that it should be accomplished with the kind of speed that it takes for a gifted person to learn a language or a clever cook to discover a new way of making pancakes. The mills of God grind slowly *because* they must grind small. Only unadvanced souls can continue to suppose that so immense a process as spiritual evolution could be accomplished in a single lifetime. No, the individual needs time to achieve its final results, and this means repeated opportunities to grapple with life. New lessons must be learned from each rebirth. We need time to acquire greater and greater wisdom in the choice of rebirths. The kind of interior, spiritual evolution with which we are presently concerned in this chapter is virtually unintelligible without both reincarnational opportunity and also an accelerated ability for making wise choices in the selection of a new womb for rebirth. Those who have entered upon this new course of evolution have already received correspondingly new powers and new responsibilities in their exercise.

Our concern for the evolution that is taking place in, and that can take place only in, the individual certainly does not absolve us from our responsibility for human survival. We all know the peril in which our crowded planet stands even apart from the hideous nuclear follies that may take place. It should be obvious that concern for the evolution of the individual implies concern for that which has cradled him. Yet the survival of the human race is important only for the evolution of the individual. Moreover, we must recognize that our planet, like everything else, will eventually die, whether it takes another thousand or another million years. This might well mean the end of the human race as we understand it, for although the colonization of other planets is not entirely unthinkable, it is far beyond all sober reckoning in the foreseeable future, not least since the rest of our own solar system is so inhospitable to human life.

Eugene Sanger, a German space pioneer, suggested that vehicles might be driven through weightless space at such fantastic speeds, aided by the pressure of radiation, that they might keep up for a year or more a speed approaching that of light. In terms of such a futuristic fancy a man and woman might conceivably get to another inhabited or at least habitable planet within a few years. They might have to abandon hope of ever seeing planet Earth again; but then the early immigrants to America generally never expected to see their homes again or the familiar scenes of their youth in Europe. So in such an updated form of Noah's ark a remnant of the human race might be spared to begin all over in outer space. Yet even if so fantastic a dream were realized, it would be

futile unless the purpose of the biological salvation of humankind were clearly envisioned: the *interior* evolution of the
individual. For man can never be *merely* an endangered
species to be preserved as we try to save certain endangered
whales. These we try to preserve for nature lovers to love and
naturalists to study. Humankind, on the contrary, serves the
individual in his or her pilgrimage only in making possible a
certain kind of milieu for rebirth and the spiritual training
that rebirth provides.

But what precisely is it that is reincarnated? Certainly not
the "me" that you casually identify as me when you happen to
meet me walking down the High Street. For that "me" is
changing and evanescent as can be seen even without any
reincarnationist hypothesis at all. It is in a constant state of
flux. Sometimes I am morose, sometimes ebullient; at times
radiant with energy, at other times fatigued. These changes
you might not notice from day to day; but if you had not seen
me for twenty years, you would doubtless notice a considerable
change. If, having seen me at the age of five, you now met me
even ten years later, you might well not recognize me at all as
anyone you had ever met. Between the new-born child and
the dying old man or woman the difference is enormous, not
only in appearance but in personality, in intelligence, in
virtually everything that could show under even the most
varied and intensive analysis. So much is this so that the great
eighteenth-century philosopher David Hume denied that
there could be anything that might be called "personal
identity" other than the stream of varied sensations that is
constantly in flux and that is called, for linguistic convenience
or shorthand, "I."

Hume was right in drawing such special attention to the
ever-changing character of that which is popularly identified
as "myself," since in truth it is as ephemeral as he said it is.
According to the teaching of the ancients of the tradition in
which Plato stood, there is a permanent self beyond what you
call *me* and I call *you* when we identify one another on the
street. We may sometimes catch glimpses of this underlying
self, especially through experience of the kind of love that

transcends self-interest: the kind of love that remains constant
when the handsome young man turns into a paraplegic and
the lovely young girl is crippled and old. Yet this "inner" self is
as elusive as the "outer" self is ephemeral.

According to the characteristic teaching of the Ancient
Wisdom, the self is represented in various forms of consciousness. Poetically, this may be expressed in terms of an onion
or an artichoke whose layers may be successively peeled off,
leaving an inner core; but in more serious philosophical
presentations it should be called, rather, a variety of aspects
or dimensions of consciousness. For the "inner" self is not
one entity in a compound of entities enduring through all
life and through all successions of lives; it is the core. Traditionally, man is represented as having seven dimensions of
being. A. P. Sinnett, for example, provided a schema rooted
in ancient Indian thought and based upon the teachings of
H. P. Blavatsky, who reawakened interest in theosophy
in the West. According to this schema, man consists of:

1.	physical body	rūpa
2.	vitality	prāna-jīva
3.	astral (subtle) body	linga-sarīra
4.	animal soul	kāma-rūpa
5.	human soul	manas
6.	spiritual soul	buddhi
7.	spirit	ātma

Of these the three last constitute the immortal essence of man.

Of course what is important in all this is neither the septuple
nor the triadic arrangement but, rather, the perception that
man is multidimensional, spanning various modes of consciousness. His various embodiments minister to his self-
understanding. At the center of all embodiments stands the
self that is reincarnated. The crassest of man's embodiments
is his physical one; yet it has an importance of its own, for
the spirit by penetrating to and experiencing life in this
physical body is enabled to rise to higher modes of self-
awareness as spirit. Through imprisonment we learn to

understand better what freedom is; through deprivation we learn how to enjoy; through distance from God we see God more clearly; through the withdrawal of divine Being (the absence of God) we learn more and more of the nature of divine Being, whose self-humbling in his eternal creativity discloses to us in a special way the nature of our own being in its participation in the divine.[3]

Through the reincarnational process the individual soul or *manas* gradually sloughs off the lower embodiments and with them the passions and desires that must be eradicated through being transformed. This soul or *ātma-buddhi-manas*, being itself an embodiment at a higher level of man's being and in a greater mode of his consciousness, may be recognized by Christians as the "glorified" or "spiritual" body to which Paul refers in his vision of the Christian hope.

By passing through an immense variety of circumstances the individual learns what it means to cope with an enormous range of challenges and so to gain a mastery over all the difficulties that can confront a member of the human race, after which he may go on to higher and higher reaches of existence and deeper and deeper self-awareness. As a man who has served in every department of a factory and so knows every facet of the entire work of the factory so well that he can stand in for any position and take over any department in an emergency, so the "advanced soul" can turn his hand to anything the human condition can offer. For he is at home in town or country, as experienced in being old as in being young, as familiar with the quiet of the cloister as with the noise of the marketplace. Do not chide him for not knowing what it is to be a woman, or her for not knowing what it is to be a man; for the "advanced soul" is likely, perhaps sure, to have been both, in the course of an incalculably long series of rebirths. No longer can it seem important to be this or that but rather to use whatever he or she is to forge ahead, to make new paths, to encompass a still greater range within the mystery of Being. The effect of such development

3. For an exposition of my thought on this subject, see my *He Who Lets Us Be* (New York: Seabury Press, 1975).

on a philosophical theology cannot but be stupendous. Its effect on the understanding of our own sexuality, which is a very practical concern for human beings, is also profound, and to this we turn in our next chapter.

8

Human Sexuality and Evolution

The Lord let the house a brute to the soul of a man,
And the man said, "Am I your debtor?"
And the Lord — "Not yet, but make it as clean as you can,
And then I will let you a better."

Tennyson, *By an Evolutionist*

Human sexuality plays a fundamental and crucial role in our spiritual evolution. It is inescapable, inseparable from the working out of the karma of every human being. For such entities as may exist on other planets the situation may well be different, but for us our sexuality pertains to the essence of what it means to be human. From one standpoint we share sexuality with all other mammals; yet human sexuality is strikingly distinctive. Whatever the type of society to which we belong and whatever the rules of that society, permissive or restrictive, our sexuality presents us with problems that are unlike anything that can arise at an animal level.

The distinctively human element in our sexuality is exhibited in the specifically human tragedies and comedies to which it gives rise and that would be impossible apart from it. The laughter and the tears that are both so distinctively human are to an astonishing extent directly or indirectly related to human sexuality. If we were a race of asexual beings, or even if our reproductive arrangements were notably different, almost none of the greatest literature in the world could have been written. What would be left of Shakespeare, for instance, if we tried to extract from his plays, comedies or tragedies, all that relates to the sexual aspect of human nature? Even children's fairy stories would have to be rewritten, depending as they do on the femaleness of witches and the maleness of ogres. The gods and goddesses of Greek and other polytheistic folklore depend on the distinctively male and female qualities, good and bad, attributed to them, giving rise to the situations—sometimes ludicrous, sometimes tragic —that are the very stuff of their celestial adventures. For at that level the deities are indubitably all too human, for all the grandeur with which they are invested and for all that they on their Olympian heights are separated from the rest of us.

Nothing in all this is surprising. For if we are at all in process of spiritual evolution we must expect malaise such as attends growing out of one condition and into another. We are half beasts, half angels, with the bestial and the angelic aspects of our nature so interwoven that the one seems inextricable from the other. As adolescents feel and look awkward, so the whole human race is in a state of spiritual awkwardness, being, as Pascal put it in a celebrated passage, a chimera. After millions of years of development, man trails in the mud even as he stretches his head with shining eyes toward the sky. Our sexuality permeates and is permeated by this immense spiritual development in which we are engaged, with some of us still making faltering steps upward and others among us far ahead.

We are so designed that the less bestial we become the richer, finer and more intense our emotions, tinged as they are through and through with our sexuality, and the more they are complicated by a wider and wider spectrum of increasingly delicate tones and moral considerations. By "moral considerations" I do not mean merely the constraints that may be placed upon us by society's rules but, rather, those that our developing sensitivities place upon ourselves. If we could return to the pre-human level of animality, we could see nothing either tragic or comic in our sexuality; but as things are with us it is both, and the more we develop as human beings the more conspicuously this is so. For it is not a question of personal immaturity or prolonged adolescence, since at the spiritual level we are all adolescing so long as we are working out our karma at the human level. Moreover, our sexuality comes in various guises, most obviously in the difference between men and women, but also in various deviancies from what is generally accepted as the norm. Such deviations point poignantly to the acute malaise of being human; but the malaise is there even when no deviancy is discernible to anyone using generally accepted behavioral standards.

That the sexuality of men and women is strikingly different is obvious, if only in the notoriously widespread misunderstandings that exist between the sexes. Each tends to think the other bereft of a dimension fundamental to life itself. Each tends to see in the other all sexuality reduced to the absurd. Each also tends to recognize in the other (at least in honest moments) that aspect of sexuality that complements his or her own limitations. On the one hand, female sexuality often seems to men so spread out, so diffuse, so saturating as to render women incapable of separating it from anything they can ever think or say or do. Men's sexuality, on the other hand, often seems to women to be so detached from the rest of a man's nature as to make it both laughably and tragically superficial: thoughtless, terrifying, volcanic, yet at the same time trivial. In greater or less degree men and women generally fear one another. They do so with some reason, since in some ways women are, as Ashley Montagu and others have tried to show and have persuasively argued, the undoubted superiors of men, so that men have been forced to devise legislation and societal conditions to protect themselves from female domination. Yet men are in other ways no less plainly better than women. Paradoxically, it is when men and women are both at their strongest and best that they stand most in need of each other. They are indeed, as nature intended them to be, each one half of a scissors.

Yet when all that is said, human sexuality, polarized though it be in men and women, is even more radically connected

with whatever it is that makes humanity human than with
what makes men men and women women. It is more, far more,
than libido. Intricately connected with art, religion, and all
that drives men and women upward to the stars, it is also that
which keeps them both firmly rooted in the earthiness of our
human condition. In sensitive men and women it intensifies
awareness of the pilgrim character of our business on earth.
The fascination of each for the other can make it seem odd
that two kinds of human being, at once so different and so
similar, should be engaged in a common karmic enterprise.

Men and women, in almost all respects not directly related
to their reproductive functions, seem to be fundamentally
similar. We digest our food alike; our stomachs, our bowels,
our kidneys, our hearts, indeed all our non-reproductive
organs function in women as they do in men. We do not need
medical specialists in diseases affecting the kidneys of women
or the stomachs of men, for here no significant differences
between men and women are to be found. Nevertheless,
through every finger and every toe, to say nothing of our
brains and nervous systems, flow our distinctive and sharply
divergent patterns of sexuality. It is indeed as though men
had been steeped in a blue dye and women saturated in a
pink one. Sexuality permeates our whole being. All our
desires, not merely our specifically sexual ones, are profoundly and intricately related to our sexuality.

From one standpoint this sexuality is an animal aspect of
humanity: that which connects us to lower forms of life such
as dogs and cats, rats and mice. From another it is precisely
that which carries us far beyond all other animals. What
animal other than man worries about environmental
problems, or nuclear war, or an afterlife? Our sexuality is at
once the prison that chains us to earth and the ladder that
leads us to heaven. Our lives, from a naturalistic standpoint,
might be said to consist of birth, copulation, and death. With
the first two the connection of our sexuality is obvious; yet
no less the case is its connection with death. Not only is this
connection suggested by modern psychoanalysts in the
Freudian tradition; the karmic principle shows us that it is

through our sexuality that we are led through death and its aftermath to rebirth.

A glance at how the Ancient Wisdom portrays the complexity of the self in its manifold of embodiments may help to exhibit the peculiar role of sexuality within it. But first let us ask in what way, within the average person's mode of consciousness, our sexuality can serve as a hindrance to and in what way it may be seen as an instrument of our spiritualization. While my sexuality gives me an awareness of my animal nature, it also calls to my attention my incompleteness. Whether as man or as woman, I am only half of what it means to be human. It is in the realization of this incompleteness that I perceive that my sexuality, although rooted in my animal nature with all the powerful reproductive drive this nature entails, raises me to a definitely higher level of consciousness. From that level I become aware of my ambivalence, my standing at the crossroads of an evolutionary development that can take me far beyond the present range of my awareness. In a person of the opposite sex I can see the same problem that I have viewed, so to speak, from the opposite side of the street, accentuating the reality of the problem and its importance. As an animal I do not have the possibility of such awareness; as a human being it falls immediately within my reach, tingeing my sexual urge with a poignancy that is peculiarly human. Even as I dig my feet into earth I soar upward to heaven.

That our human sexuality is a mystery is a commonplace of romantic literature. Let us see how the Ancient Wisdom can unravel the mystery. According to its teachings, as we saw in the previous chapter, a human being is much more than either the physical body we empirically perceive and touch or the non-spatial consciousness that inhabits or is somehow associated with that body, apparently in some measure at least controlling its actions. As we have seen too, beyond the physical body and interpenetrating it is a subtler one, sometimes called "astral." This rarefied body or field is not visible to the eye as are arms and legs, noses and eyebrows. Clairvoyant persons, nevertheless, claim easily to perceive it as fluctuating colored light extending in all directions beyond the limits of the physical body and reflecting the ever-changing emotional patterns of the individual's personality. Now he is angry, now devotional; now he is expansively merry, now concentrating on a highly intellectual problem.

Beyond this astral body is a subtler one still, called "mental" as it is associated with thought, then a "spiritual" one, each more rarefied than its forerunner. Since the nonphysical bodies or fields duplicate the organization and content of the physical body, they are capable of standing in for the latter. In other words, we may be said to have "back-up" bodies that make possible continued existence after the death of the physical body, though these bodies are not really auxiliary but an essential aspect of the self. These bodies can store the memory of the physical brain even after the latter has died with the physical body; the astral or subtle body can take over as would a back-up battery. The self or ego is there-fore never really disembodied. It loses only its outer physical manifestation. It discards this, at least for a time, as does a snake its skin, and continues in the subtle or astral body in what we might perhaps call a "naked" state.

After death, then, we gradually lose the particular personal-ity we have developed in the course of this life as one by one we shed the subtle bodies. Still, we retain our selfhood. After all, our personality has changed many times through life. I am not by any means the person I was at twenty and more strikingly still not the one I was at three. Continuity, however is preserved; I remember when I was three and when I was twenty. We may find, then, according to the Ancient Wisdom, that our new condition after death will entail a shock. It may present us with obstacles to be overcome and difficulties to be unravelled. We have been so long accustomed to the presence of the physical body that its absence cannot but create a problem of adjustment.

Such sharp changes, however, are by no means without parallel within our present lives. No doubt the trauma of leaving the warmth of the womb for the strange world outside it must have brought all of us a grievous problem of adjustment. Then at puberty when, after more than a decade of childhood, our sexuality plunges us into a new state of awareness, the problem of adjustment is notoriously difficult, entailing a long and often very painful period of awkwardness. Some, indeed, never fully recover from the shock. So we are not utterly without experience of such calls for adjustment even in the course of the brief span between birth and death. Still, the shock of losing the physical body and adapting to a state bereft of it is presumably in many cases peculiarly traumatic. As with adolescence and other adaptations, however, the extent and degree of shock varies, no doubt, with a variety of special circumstances. Perhaps a nonagenarian, despite his comparatively long habituation to the presence of his physical body, may find the transition less traumatic than would most young men and women of twenty. Who can say? No doubt each case is different from the rest.

The general view taken by those who follow the teachings of the Ancient Wisdom is that at death we fall for a time into a merciful sleep, a state of unconsciousness such as "the waters of Lethe." We then wake up in the astral body. Our primary task in this condition, apart from accustoming ourselves to the strangeness of it, is to gather together, to reassemble, and to put into perspective all aspects of our emotional life, including of course the all-pervasive sexual element. All this is by no means to be eliminated or destroyed; but it is to be transformed in such a way as to put it at our disposal for use in our future development.

Those who have lived the present life on a quasi-animal level presumably find such an adjustment extremely difficult, not least in the sexual realm, since for them it is not merely an adjustment but a violent deprivation. Those who have been exclusively preoccupied with their own ambition and greed must also suffer, being as they are, almost totally unaccustomed to even the slightest kind of self-examination or self-reflection. So the grinding and gnashing of teeth that is one of the biblical symbols of hell is appropriate for those with such a background and in such a state. They are self-tormented according to their various predominant dispositions, as is so splendidly symbolized in Dante's *Purgatorio*, where the proud are bent under the heavy loads they must carry, the gluttons teased by the inaccessibility of luscious fruits hanging just beyond their reach, and those who have given over their sexuality to mere animal lust are purified by the fire of total deprivation of their accustomed habits. The ancient Catholic prayer that the dead may rest in peace is directed to those in such states of emotional re-assessment and purification, that even in the midst of their pains they may know peace through the recognition of the importance of their purgatorial task and the joy that its fulfilment will bring.

This sojourn in the astral body can be attended indeed by the joy that comes with awareness of one's own spiritual progress. Especially must this be true of those who have already made notable advancement in the course of life in the physical body. Every noble and elevating feeling, every compassionate sentiment toward the weak, every disposition to sacrificial love that the individual has harbored during that lifetime will automatically bring aid and comfort and joy in the process of assimilating feelings and emotions in this transitional state. It is therefore by no means to be regarded as a state of punishment but, rather, of cleansing and opportunity for growth. For the spiritually advanced it can also be one of satisfaction and joy at finding oneself able to transform one's emotional problems into channels of grace and avenues to further development.

Life in this astral realm of existence eventually ends in a sort of astral death, plunging the self into the still more rarefied state of "nakedness" in the innermost dimensions of the self. This transition involves yet another adjustment. For some this may be an even more troublesome one, yet one that introduces the individual to life lived in the spiritual or mental dimension of being, unencumbered by either the physical body or by the emotional aspects of the psyche. Here once again comes a period of self-examination, this time on a still higher plane. The individual must now review the mental and spiritual aspirations that he or she has entertained and the activities undertaken in the course of life lived in the

physical body. These artistic, intellectual, and moral preoccupations and concerns must be collated and set in
perspective until the whole life's experience in terms of
mental and spiritual development has been assimilated and
readied for deployment in a new life in the physical realm.
I knew a lady who at the age of eighty was diligently trying
to learn Greek. When chided by her sister that at her time of
life she could hardly expect it to be of much use to her, she
merely smiled, knowing that nothing entailing mental
discipline or even the mere expression of an aspiration toward
spiritual or mental activity would ever be wasted. One is
already advanced when one's outlook has reached this point.

The individual, now ready for and longing for another stint
in the educative struggles of life in the physical body begins
the search for rebirth in another womb. Here once again the
individual faces a process of decision. This time it is likely
to entail the acute existential anguish that arises out of a
heightened awareness of the crucial importance of the decision that he or she must make at this juncture. The decision
is a momentous one. First there is the basic question: what
sort of life circumstances, including heredity and other environmental conditions, will be most conducive to permanent
further advancement? What are the needs that must be met at
this stage? The decision is somewhat like the decision one
might make in choosing a school or college: not one that is
too high-powered, for that would be discouraging and would
invite failure, yet not one that is too easygoing, for that would
encourage idleness and inhibit the very kind of moral and
spiritual progress whose importance has become so patently
clear to the individual facing the decision. At this point the
individual is so conscious of the importance of the decision
that even in longing for rebirth he or she may be held back
through lack of opportunity. There are so many considerations, so many points to weigh before determining the kind of
life circumstances to seek.

Finally, having decided in principle what is needed, the
individual must now search for what is available. It is one
thing to know what one is looking for, another to find it. Happy

is the soul who knows intuitively the right choice to make and who secures what is needed. Doing so is like making the right choice of a lifelong mate in marriage. It is a choice made by informed instinct, with full awareness of the difficulties and disadvantages it entails. One says, in effect: "I know all that very well; nevertheless I so choose. The choice is right *for me*." Moreover, in making the choice I am never really alone; I am, as always, "encompassed by a cloud of witnesses."

Of course such ancient and picturesque imagery is but poetry. It expresses, none the less, the nature of the process of deciding upon a new birth. The analogy with a marriage in which the partners are deeply concerned to succeed in living together creatively and constructively "till death them do part," all obstacles notwithstanding, is illuminating. For such a marriage (the kind Chesterton had in mind when he suggested that what is needed is not easier divorce but more difficult marriage), in which "the twain become one flesh," is rooted in human sexuality. Yet it draws the partners together in a lifelong adventure of the spirit that will eventually exhibit the supreme purpose of the marriage. So then can be seen the process of entering upon a new birth. It exhibits an even more radical aspect of human sexuality in which the psyche, while longing for a new physical body and the life that goes with it perceives at the same time, in proportion to his or her spiritual advancement, the higher purposes and needs of the soul as it proceeds on its long pilgrimage into higher planes of spirituality and greater dimension of existence. There is too the decision to be made concerning one's sex in the forthcoming life.

In writing of entry into a new embodiment as the making of a choice, I wish to clarify my intention. It is certainly not to suggest that the choice is at all like the kind of choice a New Yorker might make in selecting Bermuda or Maine for his vacation this year; nor is it the sort of choice one makes in going to the opera when one might go to the ballet. Such choices are generally made for somewhat arbitrary, not to say trivial reasons, perhaps even sometimes little more than the gratification of a whim or the indulgence of a mood. We are concerned here with a choice that might well be interpreted as no choice at all, in the sense in which, having carefully researched the possibilities and my needs, I choose Doctor X and Hospital Y. You might express some astonishment, seeing that many options seemed open to me, but I might be able to show the wisdom of my choice, concluding with the observation, "So you see I really had no choice"—that is, no other wise or prudent one, in the circumstances. You might say, from one standpoint, that God or "the lords of karma" dictated the choice; but since I could then reply that in effect I had left myself no other *wise* choice, I am entitled to call what I am doing my choice. Theoretically I could make another choice, but being perceptive enough to see how foolish I should be to do so I refrain from all other choices and make this one. Having painted myself into a corner the only sensible choice left me may be between huddling up till the paint dries or pole-vaulting across the patio and, since it would be imprudent for me either to walk across the wet paint or to be late for work, pole-vaulting may be all that is left to me by way of a solution. For even that option I may be grateful. Happy am I if I have so conducted myself as to make many choices available to me!

Among the choices that must be made in entering a human embodiment, one of the most obvious would seem to be between a male and a female one. That is, after all, the way in which the human race is most obviously polarized. It would seem that since maleness or femaleness is strikingly and emphatically a circumstance of one's life, the choice between them must be of crucial importance in assuming an embodiment. One might even speculate that, in those cases in which maleness and femaleness seem to be ill defined in a particular human being, there may have been an element of indecision.

This question is complicated by a consideration of Jung's plausible *anima* theory, according to which the most male of men must come to terms with his *anima* and the most female of women with her *animus*. What constitutes maleness and femaleness in the physical body is obviously easy to state;

much less certain is what may be called male and female characteristics in the human psyche. Certainly it is not what is popularly supposed. For example, women are commonly believed to be better at literary pursuits and men at mathematical ones; but this is demonstrably false, since not merely exceptional men but virtually all the greatest writers in human history were, till quite recent times, men, while it is a commonplace among educators that able women are at least as likely to be good at logic and mathematics and poor at literary and linguistic pursuits as are some of their male counterparts likely to be good at these humanistic enterprises and weak at mathemtics and logic. Women are similarly accounted, in popular generalization, more sensitive, more feeling, and so capable of greater human sympathy than men, while men are correspondingly insensitive, unfeeling, and unsympathetic; but on the contrary many women are notably lacking in such qualities while many men have them in an eminent degree. To say the least, such considerations make definition of maleness and femaleness of the psyche too shaky a ground on which to hope to establish any useful theory.

What I would suggest to be much less contestable is the notion that belonging to one or the other half of the human race does impose certain limits on the human agent. Not only do hormones impede us in certain ways; the entire circumstance of being a man or a woman is itself a restriction, no less than is, say, poverty or the parochialism of our environment. If, then, as reincarnationists generally claim, one may expect to need sometimes an embodiment among warlike people and sometimes one among peace-loving ones, sometimes into a family struggling to survive and sometimes into a well-to-do one, sometimes into an artistic milieu and sometimes into a commercial one, so surely one might expect to experience both maleness and femaleness in the course of one's spiritual evolution. In the history of religious ideas, the androgyn myth (according to which the human race was at one time not divided as now into male and female) reflects this sense of the need to experience the other side of the human condition.

Yet when all that is said, I cannot see (merely from my own personal experience and outlook) why I, being a man, should suppose a female embodiment to be *absolutely* necessary for my spiritual evolution. Of course in this I may be radically mistaken, as probably many reincarnationists would account me. I would ask, however, whether it is necessary for everyone to experience embodiment in, say, every one of the various races (yellow, black, brown, Caucasian, and others) in order to complete one's spiritual evolution. Surely not, for if so the requirement would correspond to nothing that we know in biological evolution, in which there is no question of my having to experience every form of life in order to arrive at the human race. Evolution is not, at the biological level, by any means a one-track railroad; nor can I see any good reason why it must be so in the spiritual dimension. I would emphasize, however, that in this I reflect only my own experience, with all its limitations, and my own perceptions, with all their myopia. Others, wiser than I and speaking out of a richer background, may very well take a different stance.

We may begin to see, then, in karmic history, the immense scope of human sexuality and its stupendous power. If we accept the teachings of the Ancient Wisdom on the karmic principle and its reincarnational implicate, we must surely see that human sexuality is infinitely more mysterious and profound than is commonly presented in contemporary books on sex-education. While it has much in common with the sexuality of other mammals, it is distinctively self-conscious. In human beings the intensity of the sexual drive not only provides for human reproduction with its transmission of special genetic codes; it has also much subtler functions. It contributes, for example, as is now generally recognized, to the creative development of the human psyche, including artistic and intellectual growth, intelligence and imagination. The connection between human sexuality and religion is well known and universally admitted, although the precise relationship is highly controversial. In contrast to the comparative monotony of animal sexuality, ours has a richness that might be called, by contrast, polyphonous. Along with a dominant melody it is capable of bearing, on the one hand, harmonies and counterpoint that run deep into the human psyche, extending indeed into a vast ancestral past, and of supporting, on the other hand, descants that carry the psyche to higher and higher spheres of consciousness and even to mystical union with divine Being.

The moral problems connected with human sexuality are innumerable. They seem stubbornly to resist final solution, no matter what attitude people bring to them. Free codes of sexual behavior spawn their own problems no less than do traditionally rigid ones; they merely change the character of the problems and their reference points. Modern studies have shown, too, in what varied guises human sexuality manifests itself. I am not speaking particularly of the puzzling deviant or aberrant forms, with which we have no special concern here. I allude rather to the wide variety of sexual attitudes among the most definitely heterosexual of human beings. These notoriously vary in many ways, causing misgivings, misunderstandings, and distress as well as immense enrichment. Our sexuality, for all that it has in common with that of other mammals, is peculiarly individualistic. To all who are acutely aware of the spiritual purposes of our pilgrimage, the individualistic aspect of human sexuality points to its special role in our advancement to higher levels of existence and planes of consciousness.

Religious people, in their various ways, have always recognized in some measure the connection. Certainly they did so long before Freud. With this recognition has come awareness of the importance of directing sexual drive in such ways as may best serve humanity's lofty destiny. Their solutions may not always have been particularly felicitous and in many cases, no doubt, they have been misguided. Little unanimity is to be found among informed people today in respect of the methods best adapted to attain the high goals that lie ahead of us. It is by no means our business here to discuss, much less to be involved in partisanship in favor of either the advocates of abstinence as a way to spiritual advancement or the champions of freedom as a path to that same end. Yet we ought to take into account and carefully note the complexities of the subject, since they do point us to the fundamental importance of sexuality and its relation to the spiritual evolution that is eventually to lead human beings beyond their present state to one still nobler and finer. That is why, whatever our opinions about it may be, our attitude ought to be extremely reverential.

For an understanding of our karmic destiny and our present place in working it out, we should also bear in mind the enormous spread of development that the human race encompasses. The lowest forms of human life are mentally, morally, and spiritually closer to the higher simians than they are to the most spiritually and mentally advanced members of the human race. Such indeed is the spectrum that humanity may more aptly be called a process rather than a species. The range of the expressions of human sexuality varies accordingly in terms of the degree of our development. At the higher reaches it retains all its animal force yet with other dimensions added that give it the highly distinctive character and intensity by which it transcends animal sexuality in general while still sharing in this, somewhat as solid geometry includes plane geometry too.

Reincarnation may be seen, at least to some extent, as part of what human sexuality means. For, as modern psycho-analysis has abundantly shown, the libidinal drive we call "sexual" is far more encompassing and even more funda-mental than what is commonly understood as specifically sexual urge. It includes other instincts such as the will to power. Since an enormous range of levels of attainment is embraced under the term "human," the character of the decision to choose this or that rebirth must be expected to vary correspondingly. The character of the decision will vary in quality as does the character of the desire. At the lower levels of development within what we call the human race the individual will be less discriminating, more eager to accept whatever reincarnational opportunities occur. At higher levels he or she will long no less for rebirth but will be more discriminating, more careful to try to obtain what will provide the best moral and spiritual opportunities. At the highest levels no doubt extreme care will be exercised, despite the intensity of the craving for rebirth.

Differences in spiritual maturity will also no doubt affect the temptation to accept a rebirth that seems to promise worldly advantages of wealth and power, dignity or comfort, all of which are usually irrelevant to spiritual need. Individuals who have already attained spiritual maturity will be more discerning, less easily misled by irrelevant considerations, less prone to fall prey to the temptations that beset those less spiritually mature.

The moral elitism that all these reflections implies is, of course, quite inescapable in any system that entails any concept of spiritual evolution. Nature itself, however understood, is demonstrably elitist. Not only do the fit survive; at certain stages they survive by co-operation rather than by conquest, certainly often by skill rather than brute force. At the higher stages of human development the elimination of cultural prejudice, for example, may become necessary for survival, and a deeper hold of spiritual realities may be seen as essential to averting disaster. The deepening of spirituality is the evolutionary goal even from the beginnings of life itself. It is merely that it takes very much longer than our forefathers could have been expected to suppose.

What we know today of biological evolution makes the thousands of rebirths that reincarnationists envision as part of the process of spiritual evolution seem not merely a plausible but an inevitable entailment. If it took so many millions of years to develop our primeval human ancestors, are we to suppose that a Dante or a Mozart, a Leonardo, or a Shakespeare, a Plato or a Pascal, should emerge more expeditiously? Can we really imagine that moral values and mental capacities can appear in an individual who has made them his own, all with the mere flick of a wand or the fiat of a capricious god? To think so would surely be possible only by thoroughly misunderstanding and underestimating what spiritual quality entails and, indeed, what it is. One does not become instantly wise by wishing it. Behind the presence of insight and wisdom lies a very long history.

The peculiar intonation and timbre of our human sexuality provides a clue to our place in the evolutionary process, which has not only a past but a future. Our sexuality reminds us in a poignant way of our intimate relationship to all forms of life, not least those that we have only in part transcended. The "reverence of life" principle enunciated by Albert Schweitzer (one of the most profound of spiritual insights) might not be entirely meaningless apart from evolution, but the evolutionary principle, as we shall see in a later chapter, exhibits the profundity of its significance.

Our sexuality, then, is bound up with our spiritual evolution not only in the present life but the whole chain of embodiments in our long pilgrimage. It is a very large part of what embodiment means at the human level. Yet it is not by any means the only kind of embodiment. Advanced souls, able to see beyond the blinkers of their human state and to catch glimpses of a condition between and beyond embodiments, can have at least some notion of growth in dimensions of being in which sexuality as we know it plays no part in the evolution of the spirit. So we ought neither to ignore our sexuality nor to account it essential to all existence, any more than we ought either to belittle this present life or to deem it the entirety of our pilgrimage.

9

Stages in Spiritual Development

There is a natural aristocracy among men. The grounds for this are virtue and talents.

Thomas Jefferson, *Writings*

Obstacles are sure to come, but alas for the one who provides them! It would be better for him to be thrown into the sea with a millstone put around his neck than that he should lead astray a single one of these little ones. Watch yourselves!

Luke 17.1

The word "elitist" is in ill repute today. Rightly so when it is understood as status determined by arbitrary social circumstances such as parentage or wealth. Nor is a distaste for so vulgar an understanding of elitism merely a current fashion. The notion that wealth or social position or anything of that sort can confer nobility on anyone has been pilloried by wise men from antiquity to the present day. Rabelais long ago observed that the habit does not make the monk. So, we might well add, neither does the coronet ennoble. Not the monastic habit, but holiness, is what makes the true monk; likewise only nobility of soul can truly ennoble men and women. People are rich not because of the jewelry they dangle from their bodies but by reason of the splendor of their spirits and the grandeur of their minds.

The word "elitist" comes from the same root as the Latin verb *eligere*, to make a choice. All worthwhile life consists of making choices. As we have seen, the karmic principle means nothing if it does not mean freedom of choice: karma deals us the hand; we make the plays. All moral progress implies the continual making of choices. We are constantly refining our souls, turning up the gold and throwing out the dross: or else we are letting the dross suffocate and bury us. Nowhere in the evolutionary process is there accomplishment without sacrifice or gain without loss. In the educational process, some must flunk, if passing is to have any significance. If there is any value in going to heaven, missing it must be possible. All religion that entertains the notion of salvation also entails the notion that we are saved sooner or later from an evil destiny of some kind and that we thereby attain to a good and blissful one. For to be saved is to be saved *from* something presumed to be at best undesirable and at worst horrific.

What is so horrific in the traditional Christian schema, especially in Protestantism which lacks a purgatorial doctrine, is the notion that we have but one chance: one chance in a life of indeterminate length, ranging from perhaps only a few hours to a hundred years or more. It is like an examination with neither a clearly defined time limit nor the absence of a time limit, but rather one in which at any moment I may be told to stop writing while you are permitted to go on, although you cannot know for how long. By contrast, the general tradition in the Ancient Wisdom has been that each one of us is immortal and therefore cannot die. You may attain your destination more quickly than I mine, but each one of us will get there eventually, however many lifetimes it may take. This is the general theosophical tradition. In principle it is what I think provides the best account of what ought to be our hope. Although it may take me an incalculable number of lives and much pain through my own wilfulness or sloth, I know I can get to my destination in the end. This is indeed what is affirmed in the old-fashioned Christian doctrine of the "blessed assurance," on which we shall have something to say in a later chapter. Nevertheless, I personally cannot help wondering whether one could go on for a limitless series of lifetimes talking of nothing better than golf scores and real estate deals with never a glimmer of concern for anything of any spiritual significance whatsoever and not become somehow redundant in the divine economy. This is of course a matter of opinion.

although it happens to accord with what seems to be Paul's view: a sort of conditional immortality. We who, for all our weaknesses, are sufficiently alive spiritually need have not the slightest doubt that we shall reach our glorious destiny, so without the slightest complacency we may rejoice that we are on the right track and evolving toward our goal, be the time of our journey long or short.

Christian teaching, Catholic and Protestant, Eastern Orthodox and Reformed, Anglican and Lutheran, is at one with the Ancient Wisdom in recognizing that the individual is in a state of pilgrimage and on a path where he or she must choose to gain salvation or to lose it. The choice must be made; it is the most important business of life. Moreover, Paul, no less than the ancient sages of India and the Greek philosophers, clearly envisions that individuals are not all at the same stage in the pilgrimage. As we have seen in another connection, he tells the Corinthians that he has had to treat them as "babes," feeding them with milk because they were not yet ready for solid food (I Corinthians 3.1-2). All religions recognize in one way or another different levels of spiritual advancement.

Where the mystical element in religion is stressed, the stages are often demarcated as degrees of initiation into the mysteries of union with divine Being. So the fourteenth-century Flemish mystic Jan van Ruysbroeck speaks of the seven steps of the ladder of spiritual love. Teresa of Avila, Spanish Carmelite and one of the greatest of all Christian mystics, uses the imagery of concentric rooms, of mansions and of outer and inner courts of mansions, and of gateways to holier and holier *sancta* of interiority. She distinguishes among various degrees of prayer: the Prayer of Recollection, for instance, is a kind of gateway to the closer converse with God that is attained through the Prayer of Quiet, which in turn leads to the Prayer of Union in which the whole soul is united with divine Being. The work of her contemporary, John of the Cross, a great Spanish poet as well as mystic, is well known: he sees the soul passing through various stages of spiritual progress, making first the renunciation of sense (the

Dark Night of Sense), then the renunciation of the spirit (the Dark Night of the Soul), and eventually the "betrothal" to and "marriage" with divine Being. For John of the Cross, mystical knowledge of God is produced by a love that takes its beginning from faith; but he specifically assures us that contemplation of divine Being is "secret" wisdom in that the natural operations of the intellect have no share in it.[1] This accords thoroughly, of course, with the teachings of the Ancient Wisdom and vividly illustrates what I am calling the elitist principle in religion.

We need not be particularly concerned here with the variety of ways in which this principle finds expression. That it takes good forms and bad, true and false, is to be expected, since religion is notoriously able to assume evil aspects as well as good ones. Jesus repeatedly warns against false prophets (e.g., Matthew 7.10). What we must face is the fact that if we are to take the evolutionary principle seriously, in its spiritual as well as its biological implications, religion cannot be either static or egalitarian. How can it be egalitarian when it encompasses, as we shall see in the next chapter, the whole range of life and our kinship with all of it? Egalitarianism works well in societies and clubs whose members are in fact equal in respect of the purposes and aims they have in view. It is meaningless wherever spiritual advancement is at issue. We certainly have such attainment in view whenever we talk of any process of "salvation." The notion of "salvation history" (*Heilsgeschichte*) that some German theologians have talked about (whatever we may think of the concept) exhibits salvation as an historical process. But in the life of the individual, whether we think in reincarnational terms or not, salvation is always a process and therefore must have a history. It is a process, moreover, in which something is being discarded even as something else is being appropriated. That which alienates the individual from God (in traditional Christian theology, sin) must give way to the "closer walk" with God that is the outcome of salvation. The elitist principle in religion is entailed in the very idea of the soteriological process,

1. John of the Cross, *Noche oscura*, 2, 18.

however it be conceived. Salvation is, of course, a long process. On the wide canvas we envision here it encompasses many lives.

Religion also in practice reflects degrees of maturity. Some of us are beginners; others are farther advanced. Even in the least Gnostic forms of Christianity, faith is not something that is grasped all at once, one grows in it. It implies a *kind* of knowledge. Calvin, for instance, explicitly recognized that faith is, as I have elsewhere called it, inductive gnosis.[2] That is to say, it is experimental, as is modern scientific inquiry. As the activities of a boy or girl in a school chemistry class reflect less maturity than do those of an experienced and original scientist, so there are wide differences among individuals in spiritual development. Some souls are still making their first, faltering steps, while others are "old hands" and many are somewhere in between. Indeed, the span is so obviously immense that only on a reincarnational view can one make any sense of it. If Rome was not built in a day, neither is a mature spirituality built in one lifetime. Spiritual maturity is the result of an immensely long process of development. Success is not inevitable.

That is why Christian theology, although it has been "officially" bereft of the concept of reincarnation, has laid so much stress upon the need for decision, justification, and sanctification. "Work, for the night is coming," warns an old hymn. Victory is not automatic. The pilgrim's path is fraught with peril. Demonic agencies lurk at every turn of the road, ready to stalk their prey. The pilgrim loves peace and is ever seeking it; yet the road he treads is a field of battle. Christians as diverse in tradition as John Bunyan, William Booth, and Ignatius of Loyola have recognized and emphasized this aspect of the spiritual life, in which progress, far from being inevitable, is impeded at every step along the way. Every life that has any worth in it at all is a struggle rather than a hymn. Vigilance no less than firm resolve is needed. To survive is to win a crown, for survival is indeed its own

2. In my Gnosis (Wheaton, Il.: Theosophical Publishing House, 1979), Chapter IX.

reward in so fearsome a conflict.

Only against such a backdrop does the concept of help from the messengers of God, angels such as ministered even to Jesus after the Great Temptation in the wilderness, become intelligible. Were there no such warfare and the struggle it entails, how could the dramatic intervention of divine help be seen as having the meaning assigned to it in the biblical account of human pilgrimage and destiny? That all life entails struggle is an existential "given"; it is also fully recognized in much Gnostic literature.

The neat, mechanistic, rationalistic systems of great thinkers such as Leibniz differ sharply from the biblical view. They envision a theodicy in which everything works perfectly like a Swiss clock. The biblical writers, who were anything other than rationalist philosophers, being for the most part too much involved in the day-to-day problems of living to have much time for metaphysical speculation, saw more clearly the nature of the human predicament. They knew nothing of evolutionary thought as we understand it today; but they were closely in touch with the workings of nature. They saw growth and development on every hand, in the grass, in the trees, in the animals they raised. They saw it by analogy in the history of the people. In what they saw no doubt they caught a glimpse of the evolutionary secret of all things.

Each religion has its own way of describing the nature of the process of spiritual advancement. Sometimes one gets the impression that it is a steady movement proceeding uninterruptedly without let or hindrance. Elsewhere it may be represented as provided by a divine agency in one swoop, as though the whole process could consist in a single act. The one is as much a caricature of the situation as is the other. If one probes more deeply into what the great religious teachers say, one finds that they recognize the great truth so well known in the Ancient Wisdom and in all theosophical tradition: it is through what we do that we obtain special opportunities in the future. Advancement is won, not given. Nor does Christian teaching run counter to this. Grace must be appropriated and so bear fruit in our lives. When God's hand is stretched out to snatch me from disaster. I grasp it with a cry of infinite gratitude: nevertheless, I still must grasp it. We are in many ways the recipient of invaluable aid on the way, but we walk the way ourselves. There are many gifts but no free rides, no piggybacks on the road to heaven. If there were, they would deprive us of our freedom. All religion worth its salt, including of course Christianity, is meaningless apart from this freedom.

The Judaeo-Christian vocabulary of the Bible is a particular one: the notion of election and advancement, however, are universal. In Hinayana Buddhism the adept has to overcome five "hindrances": the cravings of sense, ill will, sloth, anxiety or brooding, and perplexity or doubt. These the adept overcomes in four stages through which he progresses, known as "trances" or meditations. Through these he rises to the perception of the infinity of space and the unity of all things, then to the perception of the infinity of consciousness, then to the point where the mind is emptied of objects, and finally to a stage beyond consciousness and non-consciousness, in which there is neither the presence nor the absence of specific ideas. This requires long and arduous training and implies degrees of adeptship in which ethical and mystical progress go hand in hand.

The Sufis issued from the strikingly different background of Islam, being influenced also by Neo-Platonism, which came to them through an Arabic translation of Porphyry's lost commentary on the *Enneads* of Plotinus. Sufism emerged at an early stage in the history of Islam and soon developed a systematic training in the spiritual life. Under a *murshid* (director), the aspirant was led through "stations," which he had to pass in order to attain perfection in the love of God. Not all can hope to achieve such perfection. The higher way is not for everyone: it is for an elite and within its ranks are many degrees of attainment.

That Confucianism is highly elitist in conception and practice is well known. All Chinese religion, however, has tended to be syncretistic. Taoism and the various forms of

Mahayana Buddhism, as they developed in China, have reflected that elitism. The central purpose of Taoism came to be restricted to a small minority of adepts, contradistinguished from the mass of believers. The adepts aimed at attaining immortality by a strict regimen of meditation and a rigorously ethical life, such as was not to be expected of the masses, who engage in all sorts of superstitious practices.

What, then, lies behind the elitist theories and practices of religion? Plainly, the recognition, conscious or unconscious, of an ongoing evolution of the spirit that is just as much a basic principle of Being as is the evolution that operates in the biological dimension. This, in turn, implies some kind of built-in resistance to spiritual progress, which does not issue automatically as does the outcome of a computer operation but is exposed to many hazards, for accidentality is inseparable from all growth. Whatever obstacles and accidents may lie in the path of spiritual advancement, they are part of the nature of evolution itself. Of course these obstacles and accidents are not really causeless. Everything falls within the operation of the karmic principle or, in traditional Christian language, the permissive will of God; nevertheless, they serve no purpose that we humans can be expected to discern. They are as irrational as a silly giggle, as obstructive as an invisible wire across a pedestrian's path.

According to the Judaeo-Christian story of the fall of man from a state of perfection in which the lion and the lamb could company together in perfect harmony and peace (the Garden of Eden), human beings were created "good" but, being free to go astray, did go astray. Some contemporary analytical philosophers have asked (as did the ancients in their own way) why God could not have created human and all other beings so that they could not but do right, making it impossible that discord should ever result from their actions. Our understanding of the situation has been obscured by two different models of goodness that underlie the story of divine creation both in Christian thought and, *mutatis mutandis*, in other religions. According to one model, we are created by (or emanate from) divine Being, the Source of all Good and it is our duty to keep ourselves as pure as we were at the outset. According to another model, we are concerned with a goodness that is itself created by us (notwithstanding the help we receive from "on high") as we go along. God is indeed good in the first sense, but in creating us he enters into the struggle of created Being, bestowing on us the capacity to grow but exposing us thereby also to its hazards. This second-order goodness, as we may call it, is what we ourselves create. Only because we partake in some way of the first-order goodness of God can we engage in spiritual advancement through the creation of second-order goodness; yet we must remember that the gift of participation in the goodness of God is bestowed upon us only so that we may grow on our own. To say that it is we who must "cultivate our own garden" (each one of us) is not to say that we "do it all on our own." God gives us the "capital" for our enterprise and so a notable part of our duty consists in praising and adoring him. Our best praise of God, however, consists in working for our own spiritual growth.

It is in the course of that growth that we inevitably recognize the enormous span and immense divergence in spiritual attainment as in biological development. As there are countless beings far ahead of us in the scale of spiritual evolution, so there are many who have not attained our level, not only in subhuman forms of life but within humanity too. Our attitude toward those less advanced than ourselves is of the utmost importance for our development.

Mahatma Gandhi said that although he did not use idols himself he would never discourage others from doing so, so long as they found them useful; much less would he disparage the practice. In this saying he pointed to a profoundly important principle of religion. The wise and holy man reverences the spiritual kindergarten.

What matters above all here is that those who have been able to advance spiritually must not only show forbearance and toleration toward those still at a less advanced level; they must help them. This they may do by several means. First they must respect the efforts of those engaged at lower levels of growth. A mature scholar does not belittle the kindergarten child who is struggling with the alphabet. So let no one dare to ridicule, much less despise, the religion of another, however simplistic or absurd it may seem from the vantage point of a higher awareness and a more mature understanding. As the kindergarten child may be making more rapid strides at his level than is the graduate student at his more advanced stage, so the superstitious peasant may be making higher leaps toward God than is the spiritually advanced and thoughtful person who is in the wings spectating. To take any sort of supercilious attitude toward anyone less advanced than oneself in the spiritual domain is the most contemptible form of snobbery and far more reprehensible than any social or intellectual kind. Spiritual pride is pride's most vicious form.

That *noblesse oblige* was a well recognized concept in antiquity, centuries before the Duc de Lévis put the maxim in this form in 1808. It is a principle that governs the entire process of spiritual evolution. It is indeed an aspect of the karmic principle itself. The higher our level of consciousness, the more sensitive we become to the struggles of others less advanced on the pilgrim's path. It is not merely a question of compassion. To limit it to that would be an exhibition of spiritual pride. Although we are indeed called to be compassionate toward the weak, we are required so to love those who struggle far behind us that we actively help them while at the same time letting them work out their own salvation in their own way.

The Mahayana Buddhist concept of the role of the *bodhisattva* is an expression of this principle of spiritual concern.

The *bodhisattva* is one who has taken a specific vow to attain complete enlightenment, cost what it may and long as it may take, while simultaneously remaining active in the world of sentient beings and compassionately helping them till all are brought to enlightenment. He is portrayed in the Lotus Sutra as superior to the *arhat* or "enlightened one" of Theravada Buddhism whose concern is considered to be directed more to his own personal purification and enlightenment.

The fact that others less advanced than we may be awkward and ignorant in their way of going about things should inflame our zeal to help them rather than arouse in us any sense of superiority. The old story of the tortoise who, for all his slowness, overtook the fleet-footed hare is very much to the point here. One may be indeed advanced in the path to perfection yet grow less diligent in its pursuit and even, as we sometimes say, "rest on our laurels." Meanwhile, those far behind in the evolutionary path may move along with such steady resolve that they overtake those who not long ago seemed so far beyond them as to be impossible to overtake. There is no room for complacency on the part of anyone. The hare lost the race with the tortoise because he lost the sense of urgency while the tortoise kept it. The hare did not go backwards; the tortoise simply went farther forward and so overtook him.

Our duty, then, to "kindergarten" souls is plain. In helping them we ourselves grow and advance. This does not mean that we are called to indiscriminate care for those who are patently engaged in thwarting the evolutionary process and bringing about their own destruction. If we truly love the "babes in Christ," we shall seek not to indulge their whims but to encourage them to find their own way to evolutionary advancement as we, in a possibly very different way, have found ours. The bond of brotherhood with all living beings is sacred, but implementing it in a "big-brother" role is a delicate and difficult assignment, fraught with many perils. One can so easily turn it into a peculiarly invidious enterprise: a "playing God" in the worst of all ways.

Moreover, the battle in which we are engaged is not against merely human foes. The Ancient Wisdom has always recognized the existence of activity around us in invisible worlds: some evil agencies, some good ones. This theme, so familiar in Gnostic literature, appears in the New Testament and exhibits the nature of spiritual warfare as we must wage it. Any prowess we manifest, any victory we attain, is not to be an occasion for showing off to one another, still less for idle boasting, and least of all for deriding those who are not in the forefront of battle but are nevertheless manfully struggling with us to win it, their inexperience and their ineptitudes not-withstanding. For our central purpose is victory over the forces of evil; our individual salvation is a byproduct in which of course we rejoice with all our heart, but it does not constitute the agenda of battle.

We are united, indeed, to all beings: to those below us and to those above us in the evolutionary spiral. For all that is has its source in divine creativity; all issues from the mind and heart of divine Being. So not only am I "related" in sacred "brotherhood" with my fellow humans; I am also "brother" to beasts and angels. Hence the unity of all beings and the reverence-for-life principle we are to discuss in our next chapter. My relationship is not only with cats and dogs but with trees and flowers, even with the sun and the moon and every grain of sand on the seashore. The affinity with those who like myself have attained that measure of self-awareness that we account distinctively human is, however, a special one. They are close to me in the evolutionary spiral and share with me a common awareness. My responsibility toward them is correspondingly special. As a biblical writer puts it, "a man who does not love the brother whom he can see cannot love God, whom he has never seen" (I John 4.20. Jerusalem Bible).

We can best see the force of all this by considering an alternative view that could be set in opposition to it. If, as many suppose, the universe falls together by a fortuitous con-currence of events and without any guiding principle of intelligence behind it, then plainly there could be no con-ceivable reason why I should call you my brother, since we could have no common spiritual parentage to warrant any claim to such a relationship. I would no more see you as my brother than I would my opponent in an airplane dog fight. We might *behave* externally as though we had a fraternal relationship of some kind, as rivals habitually behave in the competitive struggles of business and other arenas of human strife; but this would be either a mere pose or else a conven-tion of the sort that politicians employ in talking respectfully of their opponents as "my honorable friend." It would have no inner significance, being no more than a tongue-in-cheek courtesy adopted to keep social machinery suitably lubricated.

By calling you my brother in any spiritual sense, I ought never to mean merely that you and I belong to the same club or other fraternity or that we have formed a contract of some kind that is celebrated with a ritual handshake. For the basis of our brotherhood is not man-made but pertains to the common origin of our human awareness, our special level of self-consciousness. This is not to be found apart from the Creative Spirit of God in whom, as Paul says to the Athenians on Mars' Hill (Acts 17.28), "we live, and move, and have our being; as certain also of your own poets have said, For we are also his offspring." Such is the Christian way of putting what is universally attested in all the great religions of the world: We are all "brothers" because we all spring from God.

The universal brotherhood of man is, then, as I have already suggested, a special aspect of the reverence-for-life principle. If dogs and cats and even bacilli are all in the stream of life that I share, so also of course are all men and women. The tie that binds us human beings together is nevertheless a special one in the sense that we are all within that particular spectrum of evolution in which we can directly help or hinder one another's growth. You can encourage or discourage my growth whether you are more advanced than I or less, because everything you think or say or do contributes in one way or another to the balance or imbalance of the spiritual realm around you. You spread health or infection wherever you go. True, the less advanced I am, the more susceptible I may be to your influence, good or evil; but by the same token the more advanced I am the greater can be my disaster if I do fall, for at that level I stand to have more to lose.

So, then, the universal brotherhood of man has nothing to do with concepts of political or social equality. A king can fall ill as well as can a beggar. Wealth is no guarantor of health. Indeed, the rich are often lamentably prone to sicknesses that the poor escape. It is in the interest of the whole brotherhood of man, however, that the strong should protect the weak, for we are all engaged in the same evolutionary development, however different the pace of our progress. At the same time, the weak have a duty to the strong, the less advanced to the more advanced, the sick to the healthy. In Japan, when a person has a cold he or she is expected to wear a mask over the lower part of the face so as not to infect others. At every level and in every situation we have a duty so to compose ourselves as not to infect others or impede their spiritual evolution.

This duty is not easy to fulfill. Those who have attained some growth in the spiritual world might face the temptation of wishing to keep the less advanced in a state of permanent moral and spiritual immaturity. To succumb to that temptation is to impede one's own growth as much as or even more than that of the others. In every one of the three synoptic Gospels is reported the saying attributed to Jesus that he who becomes an obstacle to the growth of spiritual babes would be better drowned in the sea with a millstone around his neck. He is a menace not only to others but to himself.

When all that is said, however, the fact remains that all religion, Buddhist or Christian, Jewish or Sikh, has as its major concern the evolution of the individual at a spiritual level. Institutional religion too often succeeds rather in the stultification of that evolutionary progress; but that is certainly not what the great religious teachers have sought to accomplish. Religion is about pilgrims' progress: advancement into the higher reaches of spiritual life. Where religion is bereft of this mystical engagement it is a mere carcass of itself. To put the matter in another way: the Kingdom of God, whatever it is, is not a democracy, and a recognition of the evolutionary character of all things brings into relief this fact of the chemistry of the spirit.

10

Our Kinship with All Forms of Life

The fundamental fact of human awareness is this: "I am life that wants to live in the midst of other life that wants to live." A thinking man feels compelled to approach all life with the same reverence he has for his own. Thus all life becomes part of his own experience.

Albert Schweitzer,
"Albert Schweitzer Speaks Out"

Respect for all forms of life is writ deep into Indian thought and practice, being carried to extremes among the Jains who interpret the doctrine of *ahimsa*, non-violence, with literalistic devotion. The doctrine has deeply influenced Indian tradition. Gandhi acknowledged its profound influence on his ethical outlook. While few would carry their adherence to the principle of *ahimsa* to the extremes to which the Jains go in preserving even the smallest forms of life, their attitude becomes thoroughly intelligible as soon as one recognizes the evolutionary principle behind all things.

Only the slightest reflection on the consequences of evolution will lead us to see that we ought not to value life simply on the basis of its being human or not. We are horrified at the idea of murder, which is generally accounted the worst of crimes against society, deserving the severest punishment society permits itself to inflict; yet most people think very lightly of the killing of an animal. For killing a man I may be sentenced to death or at least to a long term of penal servitude;

for killing a dog, even with cruelty, I may well get off without even a fine. True, a dog is much lower in the scale of evolution than is a human being; nevertheless, it shares with me the same stream of life that I enjoy. If I am expected, as most rightly I am, to show compassion to my weaker brothers and sisters in the human race and to help them in so far as I can, how can I dare to treat other forms of life cavalierly? Yet a bumper sticker proclaiming that "I brake for animals" is accounted by many an eccentricity.

In the long story of the development of Christian thought one very remarkable fact stands out. Except in a few recent developments far from the mainstream both of traditional doctrine and of central controversy, Christianity has been astonishingly silent on, not to say negative toward, the notion that all life is sacred. This notion, so fundamental to the traditions of Indian thought, is taken for granted in both Hinduism and Buddhism and sometimes, as among the Jains, it acquires extraordinary prominence in teaching and practice. In Christian doctrine, however, it has been almost universally ignored. This is not to say that individual Christians have not in their own way recognized it. The case of Francis of Assisi is well known. Yet he was canonized despite his love for birds and beasts rather than because of it. Most of the classic theologians of the Church, including Thomas Aquinas, have denied that animals have souls that could possibly be resurrected as is the case with human souls and some have openly ridiculed such a notion. Mormons, Christian Scientists, Shakers, and Seventh-Day Adventists are among the few religious bodies in the West to have taught otherwise. Mormons, following Joseph Smith expressly teach the resurrection of animals.[1]

Concern and sympathy for "dumb animals" is characteristic of many sensitive people in the West, perhaps more especially in the English-speaking world. Most of us wax indignant on hearing of cases of cruelty to dogs and cats and

1. On this see Gerald E. Jones, "Reverence for Life in Religion: Eastern and Western Views," in S. J. Palmer (ed.) *Deity and Death* (Salt Lake City: Brigham Young University, 1978), pp. 107-120.

horses. Yet the Church has made no clear, official pronounce-
ment on the subject.

On the contrary, the general impression one gets is that the
widespread disapproval of cruelty to animals found among
highly civilized people in the West springs from personal
sensitivity and thoughtfulness or from some other source not
in any way directly connected with the Christian Church or its
teachings. That is not at all the case with respect to humanity.
Christians have generally perceived humans as set apart by
God from all other forms of life and endowed with a soul,
which is traditionally taken to be what distinguishes men and
women from the lower animals and other forms of life.
Christian thought has always seen humanity as sacred, al-
thought it has been ambivalent regarding the relation of
Christian teaching to the kind of humanism expounded by
Socrates and notably revived at the humanistic Renaissance.
Man, so we learn in Genesis, was created in the image of God.
This has been universally acknowledged in all forms of
Christian orthodoxy and has never been denied by any im-
portant heretical body of Christians.

Such an emphasis on the sacred character of humanity,
male and female, has helped people to see something of their
own special destiny, of their duties to one another, and of their
relation to God. It has also blinded them, however, to the
wider question of the status of all living beings: mammals,
birds, fish, reptiles, insects, trees and plants. The typical
Western attitude to them was natural enough and perhaps
even inevitable before the general recognition, toward the end
of the nineteenth century, of the principle of biological evolution. For before then man was taken to be a *special* creation of
God, sharply distinguished from all other living creatures.
No doubt the "dominion" of man over the rest of creation,
explicitly taught in Genesis 1.28, helped to foster unconcern
for the lower forms of life. Yet it should have had the opposite
effect. At any rate, once the continuity of life is recognized
(and what we now know of biological development compels us
to recognize it), such exclusivism becomes untenable.

Not all forms of life are equally advanced. In the evolutionary process, however, we can see that latent powers are expressed throughout all the development of life from its simplest forms. As life develops, we see more and more sensitivity, more and more freedom of choice exercised, as well as more intelligence and imagination. At every stage of development is more of what Teilhard called "enhancement of consciousness." We have left the plants far behind us, but they are still one with us as we are with them in the stream of developing life. We dare not treat them as strangers. They, as we, are subject to the karmic principle and in the evolutionary scheme. Although we are at a more advanced stage in the development of consciousness, we can ill afford to forget that from the vantage point of a still higher mode of being we must seem at least as primitive as do plants and worms now seem to us. Moreover, how often the "lilies of the field" must put us to shame, obviously knowing as they do so much better how to conduct their affairs than we know how to conduct ours.

From all this we can easily see that if we are to treat all men of every race, color, and culture, all peoples, however primitive or developed, as "children of God," we must surely find irresistible the thesis that such respect cannot arbitrarily be confined to human beings. In the light of all that we know about evolution, our affinity with other beings must extend spiritually as it does biologically to our simian, canine, feline, equine, and other cousins. If I am to feel as I certainly do, a duty to my Chinese brother and am to expect a similar fraternal recognition from him, how can I dare to talk as though horses and dogs and cats had no destiny beyond that of amusing me or keeping me company or carrying my loads, and cattle and poultry no role in the scheme of things beyond putting food on the tables of carniverous humans? If Africans are to be called my "brothers under the skin," must not my pet cat or monkey be my "cousin under the skin"?

Albert Schweitzer had been preoccupied with thoughts such as these when one evening, in the course of making a fairly long journey on the river, his barge was slowly creeping upstream, laboriously feeling for the channels between the sandbanks. Suddenly at sunset as the barge was making its way through a herd of hippopotamuses, a phrase occurred to him: "Reverence for life." It epitomized the whole philosophy for which he had been seeking. It changed his entire view of ethics. He saw that once a person affirms the will-to-live and applies it universally, that person is acting naturally and honestly. One does not simply accept existence as something given; one experiences existence as "unfathomably mysterious." Affirmation of life is a spiritual act. "To affirm life is to deepen, to make more inward, and to exalt the will-to-live."

Schweitzer goes on to point out that "The great fault of all ethics hitherto" had been the assumption that ethics must "deal only with the relations of man to man." In fact one cannot be ethical till one finds *all* life sacred, "that of plants and animals, as that of his fellow men, and when he devotes himself helpfully to all life that is in need of help." Schweitzer came to see this ethic as comprehending within itself "everything that can be described as love, devotion, and sympathy, whether in suffering, joy, or effort."[2]

Recognition of the ethical implicates of extending respect to all forms of life does not imply support for this or that social or political philosophy. It simply calls attention to the fact that in our discussion of social and political theories and other philosophical speculations we have traditionally been working with a limited, highly artificial, indeed parochial presupposition that moral philosophy has significance only in terms of human relationships. Moralists and theologians have disputed with each other whether God should come into ethics at all. Moralists as such have characteristically insisted on some sort of autonomy for moral philosophy as a fundamentally and exclusively human preoccupation, while theologians have no less expectedly tended to insist that the brotherhood of man is inseparable from the Fatherhood of God: the one notion is an implicate of the other.

In this the theologians have been right in their perception; but they have not carried it far enough. Whatever we are to say of the relationship of God and man must be said of the

2. Albert Schweitzer, *Out of My Life and Thought*, tr. C.T. Campion (New York: Holt, Reinhart and Winston, Inc., 1913).

relationship between God and all living creatures. Paul in more than one passage (e.g., Romans 10.12) affirms that in Christ there is "no difference between Jew and Greek"; but to many of us this must sound almost as parochial as it would be to tell a Chinese that there is no difference between Dane and Swede. The point Paul was making was important in the setting of the Mediterranean world of the first century. If we were to say today that there is no difference in the sight of God between Arab and Jew, we might be making a salutary reminder. In the contemporary scenario, however, we might expect anyone making such a point to talk more comprehensively, so as to include men and women of every race, color, culture, and creed: Laplanders and Vietnamese, Ethiopians and Poles. Such modern comprehensiveness, however, is not comprehensive enough, since it excludes all forms of life on this planet that are not technically classified as human, to say nothing of extraterrestrial forms of life, whatever they may be.

Schweitzer tells us that when he was a little boy, even before he went to school, he found quite incomprehensible the notion that in his night prayers he had to pray only for human beings. After his mother had said the customary prayers with him and kissed him goodnight, he added one that he had composed for himself: "O heavenly Father, protect and bless all things that have breath; guard them from all evil and let them sleep in peace." When, later in boyhood, he had the duty of controlling a dog or horse, he sometimes used a whip and at the time felt, he tells us, like a lion tamer, intoxicated with power; but later in the day he felt bitter remorse, knowing that he could have achieved control over the animal without causing pain. Once during the Christmas vacation, while driving a sledge in the snow, he saw a neighbor's dog, known to be vicious, rush out in front of the horse's head. He felt justified in dealing the dog a sharp blow of the lash. It caught the animal's eye and he rolled in the snow, howling with pain. The dog's cries haunted Schweitzer for weeks. He could not get the sound of them out of his mind.

Reflecting on such scenes when he had reached maturity,

he could not dismiss such feelings as mere sentimental squeamishness. He found himself seeing that they pointed to a philosophical understanding of life that had been over-looked even by many of the noblest thinkers. He recalled that as a boy he had felt how little the scientists seemed to under-stand of the mysterious processes of Nature. The confident assertions about science that he found in his schoolbooks had caused him to develop a "positive hatred" of these books, which seemed to do nothing but go into fuller and more complicated *descriptions*, palming them off as explanations but in fact only making the mysterious more mysterious than ever. Even in these early years he had seen that what is called "life" remained to him unexplained. Only in later years did he develop his view of the unity of all life.

What we now know of the evolutionary process precludes talk of humanity as though it were a separate species in some way essentially different from all others. Man has indeed some striking features not present in other forms of life; but the traditional practice, in the West, hallowed by centuries of Christian usage, of calling man immortal and all other living creatures mortal is completely without any kind of justifica-tion. There are immense differences in development between, say, a worm and one of the higher simians. Nevertheless, the differences between individual humans is infinitely more striking. The difference between a Goethe or an Einstein, on the one hand, and a mental and moral moron, on the other, may look to the superficial eye less noticeable than the dif-ference between a dalmatian and a cocker spaniel, but in fact it is incalculably great. Even within the same family may be found a stupid, immoral oaf alongside a budding genius and saint. The brother of a Mozart may not know the difference between "Clementine" and "When Irish Eyes are Smiling." Some of the higher mammals show, by contrast, astonishing intelligence, profound sensitivity, and a noble fidelity. But for a doctrinaire view, held for centuries in ignorance of biological evolution, who could have dared to talk of "dying like a dog," that is, of simply rotting in the ground? How could the Book of Common Prayer and other Christian liturgies have confined to human beings only the promise of resurrection to eternal life?

Our kinship with all living creatures causes many people who have become aware of it to refrain from eating the flesh of other animals, not merely on health principles but because it seems to them almost like cannibalism. Regard such matters as we may, how can one dare today to make that arbitrary and sharp distinction, ingrained into the Western mind, between humanity and every other form of life? Not only must we learn to eschew it; we must face the fact that as, in the old fable, the tortoise overtook the hare, so some porpoises and chimpanzees may in the long run outstrip many humans. It is surely macabre to have to admit that, at least in theory, devout Christians have felt they ought to pray for the soul of their fellow-Christian Adolf Hitler but must refrain from praying for a faithful dog on the ground that the latter has no soul. Kindness to dumb animals is beside the point, not least since we humans are so notoriously cruel to one another. The Book of Proverbs, one of the later books of the Bible, recognizes that "The virtuous man looks after the lives of his beasts, but the wicked man's heart is ruthless" (Proverbs 12.10). Such prudential wisdom is a far cry, however, from what the case now demands: the recognition that, if we are to talk of the "souls" of men and women, we cannot deny that all forms of life have "souls" and that the difference is at most but one of development.

Historically, the emergence of the view that humanity is a special and radically different form of creation should not surprise us. So astonishing are the specifically human powers and distinctive characteristics (e.g., speech and conceptualization, tears and laughter, imagination and memory, self-awareness and worship) that human beings, in becoming conscious of them, could not but at first be intoxicated by the discovery. So the tendency to see ourselves as a breed apart and to emphasize what separates us from other forms of life rather than what unites us to them is natural. We should not remain permanently intoxicated, however, by the discovery of our human distinctiveness; the time has come for us to be no less impressed by the unity of all life.

Ethical problems arising from special cases concerning the right to kill certainly do not disappear when we adopt a reverence-for-life philosophy. Schweitzer himself recognized that in the course of his medical work in Africa he was daily engaged in the slaughter of millions of bacilli and other bacteria. Even with no medical intervention at all, our own bodies are constantly engaged in total warfare with bacteria that otherwise would destroy them. One might ask me: by what right do you kill the pneumococcus that has entered your body? Has not it, on a reverence-for-life view, the same right to life that you claim? Is not it hypocritical of a human being to pamper a poodle yet slaughter the flea that annoys it? Would not the flea, if it could have any say in the matter, be justified in an outburst of righteous indignation at human complicity in its murder?

Such problems are but an extension, however, of the familiar ones that arise in conventional ethical discussions when proponents of pacifism argue against the possibility of a just war and opponents of capital punishment insist that society can have no right to take a human life. Adopting a reverence-for-life view does not radically change the issues; it merely extends the field. It does raise, however, a new question about our hierarchy of values. On the one hand, if you think the man who killed your son ought to be judicially executed, why should he who deliberately shot and killed my dog go free or at most be fined a few dollars? On the other hand, since even a Schweitzer spent much of his life killing billions of unreflective bacteria who could not except jocosely be said to have vicious, murderous intentions in invading their hosts, need we be so squeamish as many thoughtful and sensitive people are at the idea of inflicting capital punishment on, say, a Jack the Ripper? If we have no qualms about using an anti-bacterial mouthwash to combat invading germs, why should we demur at defending our homeland with tanks and gunfire to repulse an invading army?

The problems are notoriously intractable. A reverence-for-life view does, however, put them into a different and more illuminating perspective. No sensitive person can be in any doubt that wanton attack on any living creature is by any reckoning morally reprehensible and may be a monstrous and outrageous crime. Yet the plea that there are victims' rights as well as assailants' is not to be ignored and the force of it is much clarified in a reverence-for-life philosophy. For questions of rights always imply (though the implication is too often forgotten) questions of duties. Moreover, we can become so afraid of "playing God" that we become incapable of serving him. While the plainest of duties is that of helping and encouraging those at a less advanced stage of evolution than are we, we have also the duty to protect and conserve the labors of others and of ourselves in bringing about evolutionary advancement, biological, mental, or spiritual. The widespread moral perception in contemporary society that aggression is wrong but defense right is not far off the mark, despite all the intricate problems that remain. Nature does not by any means provide us with the final word on ethical problems, but she does give us some sound hints.

For us who have become aware of a still deadlier warfare in the spiritual dimension of being, further considerations arise that put all such problems in an even wider spectrum. The author of the letter to the Ephesians (most modern scholars do not attribute it to Paul) warns his readers in a peculiarly interesting passage that "it is not against human enemies that we have to struggle, but against the Sovereignties and the Powers who originate the darkness in this world, the spiritual army of evil in the heavens. That is why you must rely on God's armor, or you will not be able to put up any resistance when the worst happens, or have enough resources to hold your ground" (Ephesians 6. 12-13). Warfare is endemic to all participants in the evolutionary process. What we have to discover is, in the language of piety, how to distinguish God's enemies from his friends and therefore know who ought to be our friends and on whose side we must fight. Reverence for life must not lead us into acquiescing in evil or submitting to the powers of darkness.

Moreover, if, as some have theorized, intelligent life on

earth may have been spawned millions of years ago by intelligent beings in another part of the universe. we should have to reckon with the special relation in which we might stand to forms of life in outer space that may be friendly or hostile to us as human beings. The moral implicates of any such speculative theory involving extraterrestrial life are profoundly mind-boggling. Yet at the same time they direct our attention to the ludicrous narrowness of traditional forms of moral philosophy. Whatever may be the forms of life that lie beyond our present empirical observation. we are likely to owe at least some of them a debt of gratitude incalculable in terms of any conventional theory of moral obligation.

The ecological concern that has increasingly affected the outlook of many thoughtful people in the last decade or two is a welcome sign of growing awareness of the value of life in all its forms. As with other similar movements. its proponents are not always as well informed as they might be. People do tend to become faddish if not fanatical on subjects of this kind. Nevertheless. the importance of ecological concern with the conditions now prevailing on our planet can hardly be exaggerated. Our environment is being polluted in innumerable ways. many of them too familiar to need mention. Through technological interference with the balance of nature we have often succeeded in producing the opposite of what was intended. The use of pesticides. for instance. has actually created pests. A typical case history is as follows. A certain species of mite is declared a pest and a pesticide is used against it. This pesticide kills off the mite's enemies who have been eating the mites. The mites. now relieved of the burden of their foes. prosper. developing an immunity to the pesticide. A more potent pesticide must then be used against the mites. This stronger pesticide proves to be also a potent carcinogen. disabling and destroying higher forms of life. including of course humans.

Ecological problems are notoriously complex. Without technology not only do big fish eat little fish by the billions daily; infant mortality among humans has been of fearsome proportions. During much of the nineteenth century it was quite common, even in the most advanced of human societies, for the majority of members of a family of ten children to die in infancy. Now, through vastly improved medical knowledge and skill, that has been changed. Through technological interference, however, we have created a terrifying array of new problems, problems that could result in making our planet uninhabitable *even apart from* the hideous danger of nuclear disaster.

All this and much more is too well known to need elaboration here. We face a practical dilemma: without technology our lives would be immeasurably impoverished, yet with technology we may be headed for holocaust. By the time we learn better, the hour may be too late. The environment we inherited may be so permanently damaged that the highest forms of life our planet has known may be destroyed and comparable ones discouraged from development.

The nostrums proposed are legion. The root of the trouble lies in a lack of reverence for life in all its forms. Yet even if motivations could be changed overnight, the problem would not be solved. Reverence for life is not a program that can be put forward and achieved by good will alone. If we take evolution seriously as we certainly must, we cannot hope to organize the forms of life and deal with them as if each were a constituent member with political sovereignty of a body such as the United Nations. The reverence-for-life principle presupposes that all life is in process of evolution. There is no absolute, unalterable demarcation between one species and another.

Competition, moreover, is inevitable at all levels. At the higher reaches the forms of life become abler in outwitting other forms. Otherwise we could not tame horses and other animals as we have done for millennia, molding them to our services. Yet the higher forms of life are for the most part more delicate in other ways, more susceptible to danger. I am more intelligent than a tiger, yet I am no match for him at all in face-to-face combat. Indeed, I am no match for a brawny, twenty-year-old moron with a lust to kill me. Wise indeed, then, is the counsel of Jesus: "Remember I am sending you out like sheep among wolves; so be cunning as serpents and yet as harmless as doves" (Matthew 10.16). Development entails the selection of qualities that have already evolved in the process of life. The right selection at the higher reaches of evolution is as necessary for spiritual health as ever it was at the lower levels for physical survival.

The reverence-for-life principle remains full of paradox, leaving us with seemingly insoluble ethical conundrums. Given the choice of being able to save organism A or organism B, how do I determine which to save? If we say roundly that all living entities are equally sacred, since all partake in the stream of life, then whether I save the pneumococcus or its host cannot be of any fundamental importance. If, however, we try to create a hierarchy of values, who am I to choose between, say, a horse and a dog, a bird and a fish? If I am to make such a choice at all, surely it will be in terms of what the species is reputed to do from the standpoint of us humans. So I may choose to kill a fly that is annoying my dog or a wasp that is about to attack my child, and surely I will have no qualms at all about destroying bacteria that are endangering me. I certainly would not entertain for an instant, however, the notion that I could be justified in killing, say, a competitor for a position we both desired, on the ground that I believed I could do more good in it than could he. Were I to prefer a horse over a dog, it could only be because of its greater usefulness to me in my present situation or to humans generally or for some other anthropocentric reason.

Again, is even human life uniformly valuable? Has a criminal lunatic as good a claim to survival as a saintly genius? Given that the choice is forced upon me to spare one and sacrifice the other, would I be morally justified in tossing a coin to decide? Few would toss the coin; yet making the choice on any other basis presupposes a criterion for the choice. In such a clear-cut situation probably few people would have any doubt about preferring the survival of the saintly genius. When it comes to a choice between two children, however, whose tendencies and capacities are still largely unknown, the choice would be much more difficult. In the case of unborn children the difficulty is extreme, since no one can predict with any certainty at all how the child will turn out. Hence the acuteness of the problems relating to abortion and other such ethical questions. Such have been the circumstances of many of the greatest figures in human history that they would have been prime candidates for abortion. By the standards fashionable in some circles today, Jesus would have been a particularly likely candidate.

The question is plainly a very practical one in our contemporary situation. We know something of the dangers attending any kind of tampering, by scientific experiment, with the genetic code of human beings; but now biologists see the possibility of a radically new and speedier type of evolution chosen and directed by man. Eric Mascall, a noted English theologian whose early training was in science, observes, in a *reductio ad absurdum*, that "by such means a dictator might insure that the next generation would consist exclusively of children fostered by himself on mothers of his own selection."[3]

Yet if, on the other hand, in deference to the reverence-for-life principle, we were to encourage indiscriminate breeding, we could very soon attain, at least theoretically, a population whose size would be catastrophic for human survival. Taking the female population of the United States of America at, say, 120 million and the span of a woman's fertility at, say, thirty years, the population of this one nation could rise within half a century to a size greater than the current population of the entire planet. Apart therefore from all other ethical considerations, restraint in population growth is an absolute necessity, on the one hand, while, on the other, all artificial methods of retarding or directing population growth raise the spectre of manipulation in this or that interest or in support of this or that criterion of selection. Then again, apart from such artificial procedures, wars and genocides have generally tended to kill off the flower of the world's manhood, the

3. Eric Mascall, "A Theologian's View of Science," *New Scientist and Science Journal*, August 19, 1971.

most promising no less than the dregs. Societies tend to destroy what they most value. In Oscar Wilde's celebrated phrase, "each man kills the thing he loves." The two qualities most prized in medieval society in the West were chivalry and holiness; the knights were killed off in battle and the monks were vowed to celibacy.

The essence of the reverence-for-life principle is that life is one. This means that I am and must see myself as in the same stream of life as cats and canaries, pneumococci and chimpanzees. My brothers and sisters include not only Armenians and Finns but, as Francis of Assisi perceived, donkeys and sparrows. In light of such considerations all killing is fratricide, for all forms of life are my kin. My identical twin is no more and no less my brother than is the blackbird on the tree outside my window. To distinguish humankind from what the Victorians called "the lower creation" (as though an eternal gulf separated us from them) is a parochial narrowmindedness, no less pernicious than the most insular form of patriotism.

When all that is said, however, we still have to face the fact that in the evolutionary process not all forms of life can survive. On the contrary, the vast majority of living entities seem to perish in the process, leaving only the specially "successful." We see this over and over again in the earlier stages of evolution. Even while one crustacean is eating another, yet another is eating the first. At the higher level that we humans have attained, although similar behavior persists, we find the beginnings of a new attitude of forbearance, toleration, co-operation and constructiveness, and of a creative kind of relationship peculiar to humanity. Recognition of the reverence-for-life principle has a salutary effect on our ethical awareness, discouraging the parochialism of traditional forms of ethics, not least those of the "social contract" type. It gives us a better perspective of the moralist's task and may perhaps even remove some traditional ethical preoccupations. It certainly will not make the moralist's task easier. On the contrary, it will pose some exceedingly difficult ethical problems. That, however, is what happens when any great new insight confronts people who are willing to accept its moral challenges.

11

Evolution and God

All growth that is not towards God
Is growing to decay.
George MacDonald,
Within and Without

If there is anything that the biblical writers clearly say or pre-suppose it is that we humans are made "in the image of God." In one way or another all religions say something of this kind. But what does it mean? Surely it is a way of saying that there is something very special about us. We are *like* other animals. We eat our food and digest it much as do other mammals and we reproduce our kind in very much the same way as they do; yet the difference between me and a dog or a sheep is far more startling than any similarity. Whatever that difference may be, it provides me with a clue, however modest, however tenuous, to the nature of God. God is not merely the principle of the birth-copulation-death cycle that we find in the farmyard but must encompass in some way those precious human qualities such as compassion and those marvellous human powers such as the use of symbolic speech in human language. To say, then, that I am "in the image of God" does *not* mean that my dog is not at all "in the image of God"; it does mean that I am "in the image of God" in such a special way that I can be conscious of having a clue to the nature of

God that would not otherwise be available to me. Through awareness of my distinctive humanity I become conscious, dimly though it be, of the nature of the divine Being who makes that humanity possible.

As soon as we have tried to clear the ground about what we mean or think we mean in using the term "God," we find that what we are in fact discussing is God's nature. As we become dissatisfied with this or that understanding of the divine nature, we propose another; theological controversy develops; sides are taken; schools of thought emerge. Notoriously such controversy often tends to be as unprofitable as it is acrimonious. The acrimony might matter little if only the discussion showed any sign of issuing in a decisive result or at least in a result as decisive as could be expected in terms of present human capacity and development. This is the case with the results of scientific inquiry in such areas of human knowledge as come under the domain of, say, physicists and chemists. On the contrary, however, the more erudite the discussion of religion and the keener the philosophical acumen with which it is pursued, the more hopeless often seems the possibility of a satisfactory and convincing outcome. Biblicists will fall back on the Bible as revealing the truth about the nature of God; but this only begs the question of how the Bible is to be interpreted and the extent (if any) to which it is to be taken as normative. For there is certainly no way of reading anything without at the same time interpreting it in one way or another. Biblicists may then appeal, as traditionally they do, to the *testimonium Spiritus Sancti*, the testimony or witness of the Holy Spirit of God, who is his own interpreter; but the fact remains that more must be needed, since two readers, each as sincere as human beings ever are, may come away from the Bible with very different understandings of its message.

Let us take a simple example of the kind of controversy that develops. In the history of Western thought one of the sharpest partings-of-the-way has been the cleavage that has been held to lie between what came to be called, in the seventeenth century, "pantheism" and what came to be sharply

contradistinguished from it as the "biblical" view. This sup-
posedly "biblical" view was that God, although he acts in
human history, stands so apart from his creation as to be
fundamentally separate from it and therefore from all that is
human. He is therefore more properly designated as "The
Other" than as the "All-in-all." Because of this prevailing
view, a thinker such as Spinoza who could talk of "God or
Nature" (*deus sive natura*) could not but seem notably heretical.
Mystics such as Eckhart were likewise to be accounted somewhat dangerous although, like poets, they might be excused
on the ground that with a little exercise of Christian charity
they might be deemed theologically irresponsible.

With the intellectual scenario so set up, the entire realm of
nature was seen in sharp contrast to God. Nature itself must
be God's creation, and so when we study it as scientists do
we are studying the created order, not God. That was indeed
the function of scientists: to mind their own business, namely,
the study of everything other than God. The problems
generated by positing such a dichotomy had arisen in Islam
before they had begun to trouble the Latin Christian West.
Christian thought in the Middle Ages inherited the problems
as they had confronted the Muslim thinkers in the Golden
Age of Islamic thought.

When an unbeliever denied the existence of the biblical
God, he seemed to be setting up and deifying Nature in God's
place. That, in such a scenario, was plainly idolatry if not
blasphemy. The scientist who could not see the biblical God
as the creator of Nature was focusing upon something created
and in effect calling that creation God; that is, he was seeing
Nature as "Ultimate Reality." Did not Genesis clearly say
that God created not only the sun and the moon but light and
darkness? Then must not the believer sharply distinguish God
from everything else? Poets like Tennyson could talk of
seeing God in flowers in crannied walls, but such talk, being
mere poetic conceit, merited no official recognition in serious
theological inquiry. On the traditional view, as we have seen,
poets and mystics are not to be treated seriously. They are
merely the ornaments of Christian culture, not its mainspring.

If, however, we go back to those portions of the Bible that express a primitive Hebrew outlook, we find a different way of looking at questions of this kind. We look in vain for support for one side or the other in a religion-versus-science debate, as we look in vain for an outlook that presupposes the kind of sharp opposition between soul and body, between "spiritual substance" and "material substance," that emerged in and for long remained a basic presupposition of European thought. In that primitive Hebrew outlook, God "rides upon the storm." His voice is heard in the thunder. Yet, as the psalmist proclaims, "the heavens declare the glory of God" and they include, of course, such phenomena. God's will, moreover, is seen in human history. These early biblical writers could no more have raised the kind of question that Western philosophers and theologians eventually came to raise than they could have discussed questions about oxygen and hydrogen. What they did see plainly, however, is that phenomena such as wind and calm, fire and earthquake, light and darkness, encompass more than can be seen or touched. Behind, beyond, and within them is a wonder greater than they are in themselves: a wonder that is not seen as light is seen, or heard as wind is heard. Here indeed lies the astonishing power of the Bible as a literature that mysteriously captures a dimension of Being that goes beyond all that we can ask or seek or think, yet deepens our experience of all that we ever see or hear or smell or taste or touch.

Whatever the early biblical writers say, they could have seen nothing of a dichotomy between "religion" and "science," between God and Nature. The Hebrews had no word for Nature. So of course nothing that these writers say could warrant such a dichotomy, which arises only from a later development in human thought. Wherever such a dichotomy is found by those who claim to be guided by the Bible, those who make it are reading into the Bible more than the insight into the nature of God that it reveals. Wherever "science" and "religion" can be happily married without injury to our perception of God, we may be sure that we are at least on track and may therefore hope to understand whatever it is that is revealed in the Bible.

Of course by no means all or even most of the scientists who perceived the evolutionary nature of the development of life thought in terms of any kind of spiritual evolution. Certainly not all evolutionists have been interested in the question of God in relation to the concept of evolution. One of the problems in the theories of evolution that first came to the general attention of the public in the nineteenth century was that of what was popularly called "the missing link": the inability of such theories to give a convincing account of the transition from one level of biological development to another. Darwin talked of variations among members of a species, De Vries of mutations as conditioning certain members of a species to possess variations that favored survival. Neither satisfactorily explained by what means the variations could and did occur. Darwin and De Vries both seemed to assume that a change occurred in some *part* of the organism, either gradually or by a sudden "jump" or "leap." Organisms, however, have a functional unity such that one must expect a variation in one part of an organism to have concomitant variations in all its other parts. How then could there be successive changes of form yet a continuity of function? According to those who took a Lamarckian view, certain organisms made a peculiarly strong effort that enabled them to develop capacities favorable to survival; but how could the results of such an effort be genetically transmitted to subsequent generations? Spencer offered a theory of the transmission of acquired characteristics, but this was accounted by many quite unconvincing.

The notion of "effort," however, was on the right lines, as Bergson saw in his theory of the *élan vital*, the vital impulse, that drives all organisms *constantly* toward more complicated and higher modes of organization. This drive may be impeded in various ways, but it is always there; it is as much a part or aspect of life itself as is the sexual or any other biological drive. It is the creative power within life that is ever moving it in an evolutionary direction.

Our intellect (computer-like power that it is) stops the flow, so to speak, and analyzes what it sees when the flow is stopped. As we might say today, it stops the cinematic continuity of the moving picture and produces a still, which may be very useful for a variety of purposes but nevertheless destroys what is most fundamental to a moving picture, namely, the continuity of its motion. So in Bergson's theory of laughter (in *Le Rire*), a sudden stoppage, making a still picture where we expect the movie to go on, produces an effect that is either funny or artificial or in one way or another startling and "unreal." An extreme example would be the miraculous stoppage of a bullet in the course of its trajectory. What the intellect does is to distill from the stream of life certain ingredients that are susceptible to its computer-like powers of analysis. This is, of course, immensely useful, but it does, as I have already suggested, tend to mislead us into thinking that it gives us a model of reality when in fact it destroys the reality as surely as we destroy the reality of a living organism whenever we kill it and cut it into pieces.

The importance of such considerations is that, while through intellectual analyses we get a picture of evolution as a single line upward through measurable levels, there is indeed no such line and are no such levels but, rather, a variety of divergent tendencies at work.

Two opposing views may be taken by those who see God as in some way involved in this constantly creative process. On one view, divine Being itself *is* the process, so that if we are to talk about God at all we must see divine Being itself as evolving, since that is the nature of all being. On the other view, God, although he is by his own will and loving purpose involved in the creative evolutionary process at every point and therefore may certainly be said to be "in" it, is nevertheless at the same time the principle and the spring of the process. On this view, without such a principle behind the growth, the growth would be "wild," so that the whole universe would be a gigantic cancer. God is to be seen as independent of the process and so "beyond" it and worshipped with the kind of adoration that such a status surely demands. So he is indeed "The Other." He is the Being whence all other being flows in the creative process he eternally initiates. Both Aristotle in the ancient world and Whitehead in our own century have seen, each in his own very different way, such a vision of being and becoming, of reality and process, although the vision of neither of these thinkers will fully satisfy all religious insights.

The sharp dichotomy that seventeenth-century and later theologians have made between what they called a "patheistic" view of God, on the one hand, and, on the other, a deistic or theistic one, is no longer usefully made. We must do justice to both views. I believe we can do so in seeing God as the principle and fount of the eternal creative process, beyond it, dwelling in a realm of "light inaccessible, hid from our eyes," and nevertheless also in its midst, bespattered with its mud, at every point saturating it with his love and enfolding it with his care, yet leaving it always open and free so that all that the creatures achieve shall be their own accomplishment, although only his superabundant grace has made that accomplishment possible.

Evolution proclaims, then, that God is *both* utterly beyond his creation and *also* within it wherever the creative process is. He knows the hairs of our head; not a sparrow falls to the ground without his knowledge. Such is his love that he groans with us in our sufferings and dances with us in our joys. All this is possible because we are always in process of growth while he is the principle thereof. Whatever we are that is of value he must be *par excellence*. That is why he must encompass, for example, all our personal values as well as all impersonal ones and must therefore be acclaimed as personal, for all that theologians may insist that he is suprapersonal rather than personal. That is why we ought to adore him in what must seem to the uninitiated the groveling of a slave to a despot, while at the same time we greet him as within us, for "Closer is He than breathing, and nearer than hands and feet." To perceive the evolutionary process in a spiritual perspective *is* to know the nature of God as both deep within us and utterly beyond us. "God moves in a mysterious way"; yet the principle of evolution gives us the key to that way and therefore to God's nature.

The principle of evolution sheds light not only on the way we develop, mentally and spiritually as well as biologically, but on the nature of God as the fount and principle of that development as of all else. For God can no longer be seen as a wand-waving creator who produces whatever he wants by a simple, not to say capricious, assertion of his will. Nor can values be measured as though they had come ready-made out of God's hands. No, whatever is to be valued has evolved and is evolving according to the evolutionary principle that is the gracious Being of God at the heart of all things and that entails sacrifice, effort, and hurt, at every step of the way.

That God is love is the message that is surely at the core of the Bible, not least at the heart of the Gospel. An evolutionary understanding of the creation of all values helps us to see the cost of creation and therefore the loving nature of the Creator who accepts that cost. This surely is what is to be understood as the eternal principle of sacrifice that is expressed in the Christian doctrine of the centrality of the Cross, with all its sacrificial implicates. The eternal values are not values on a scale by reference to which we humans prefer diamonds to glass or silver to bronze; they are values on the scale of the sacrificial love they entail. I stand in awe of a saint because I know (or can at least perceive something of) the cost of his or her becoming that saint. The price is measured not only in terms of what that saint has "paid" in the process of his sanctification, but in terms also of the cost of the divine love that made that sanctification possible. When you have seen my part in my sanctification, such as it is, you have seen only one aspect of its cost. For I am only, so to speak, a tenant farmer in the vineyard. God has provided the land for me to cultivate, with the rain and the sunshine that are indispensable for my success. The use I have made of these gifts has developed me and, through the operation of the karmic principle, has provided me with the opportunity to advance myself further still. Yet if you want to see the total bill for the project, you will have to go far beyond what I personally have paid. You will see a vast evolutionary history in which God has been and is constantly at work, constantly involved, constantly suffering not only in and with his creation but far beyond what his creatures could ever possibly know.

To see evolution as some of the Darwinians and Spencerians saw it in the flush of their nineteenth-century excitement, is to see only a fragment of the process. Evolution not only tells us something of the origin and development of hominids from their mammalian and more distant ancestors; it is the key to an understanding of how everything that is comes to be. Everything that exists is in one way or another produced by development and growth. Yet not all growth is of the same order. A puppy does not grow exactly as does a bush or a flower; nor does a child grow exactly as does a puppy, for in the child is a dimension that transcends what we can ever expect of a dog. The hand of God is in everything; yet its effects are not perceptible in the pup *in the way* they are in the child who is developing powers of reason and spiritual sensitivity beyond what could be expected of any dog.

We have seen that one way of expressing this (a traditional Judaeo-Christian one) is to say that man is made in the image of God; another is to say that God breathes something of his own *ruach*, his own breath, his own Spirit, into man. God, however, breathes his Spirit into all his creation, so we ought surely to say, rather, that in man he does so in a special way. God makes possible man's development of those qualities that we associate with the human state, such as, for instance, compassion and thoughtfulness, and those powers such as the ability to symbolize concepts and to use symbols in the speech that is characteristic of human language, contradistinguished from the mere chatterings of monkeys, the chirps of birds, and the grunts of pigs. The evolutionary principle applies everywhere in the universe. The chemical constituents of my body are fundamentally akin to those found in rats and mice. All life is continuous. Nevertheless, the principle as it applies to such rodents applies to me *sublimiori modo*, to borrow a medieval phrase; that is, it is to be seen in a grander, more sublime manner. I do not feel that my human dignity has been denigrated by my kinship with rodents and other forms of life in other stages in the evolutionary scale. On the contrary, the reflection calls to my attention both the enormous development that has occurred between the rodents and myself and the extreme improbability of my representing the ultimate peak of evolutionary development. I am therefore made more than ever aware both of my own worth (including the cost of the staggeringly long and arduous process of development that has made that worth possible) and also of the infinite range of growth that lies ahead of me.

Much more than all this, however, is implied in this awareness of my place in evolution. For with it is given me the awareness that I certainly have not reached my present state entirely unaided. On the contrary, it has been accomplished over the course of millions of years in, with, and through the activity of God at every point in the process. Never has God failed to be somehow involved in the process; never have I been without the direction of invisible helpers; never, in short, have I been alone. No one has done the evolving for me, for no one can ever do anyone else's growing. Yet by infinitely patient suggestion, by relentless pursuit of me "down the arches of the years," as Francis Thompson expresses it in *The Hound of Heaven*, by placing me in this circumstance and in that through the working of karma, as I have earned by my actions, no matter how long my education should take, God has accomplished the miracle of such schooling as I have so far been able and willing to accept and to assimilate. Most startling of all, I have learned at last to see God as the focus of the process of my growth and its spring. In traditional Christian language I have been "converted," that is, turned towards God.

Awareness such as this *entails* knowledge of God's nature. That does not mean, of course, that the entailment of such knowledge of the nature of God exhausts what is to be known of his nature. As has been often pointed out in one way or another by classic theologians, a God whom we could wholly comprehend would be no God at all. Nevertheless, my awareness reveals to me what God is in the sense that I can see how he works, and when one sees this one sees the nature of the worker. The psalmist could say that "the heavens declare the glory of God"; but more wonderful by far than even the galaxies in outer space, which evoke our awe and whose magnitude surpasses our human capacity to grasp, is the inner power of a single soul, even a primitive one, to say nothing of that of a Goethe or a Leonardo. In such a soul is "declared," in a louder and clearer way, that glory of God that the psalmist, even with a very limited understanding of astronomy, could see in looking at the stars above him.

What we learn above all of the nature of God is that divine Being is gracious and creative. The values he creates are not mere artefacts in a sculptor's exhibition or paintings in an artist's gallery, which are beautiful or interesting to look at but can be destroyed more quickly by fire or earthquake than ever they had been executed. On the contrary, the values God creates are imperishable, woven into the eternal fabric of his eternal evolutionary design. He accomplishes whatever he does through the karmic principle, making his creatures free: free to make or mar their destiny, and above all free to learn from their own mistakes. For the evolution we discern is moral. At the lower reaches the moral nature of the karmic principle is less obvious, less discernible; yet when seen as part of the process that eventually brings forth a Dante or a Mother Teresa it can be seen as part of the enormous cost of spiritual growth. God, who is the mainspring, the inner principle of this growth and therefore beyond it, is also in it, with it, and through it.

The karmic principle, which is at the root of all things and an aspect of the nature of divine Being as righteous and loving, exhibits itself to us humans in our own development and the problems we face in our spiritual growth. In this development we may not "see God"; but we do get a striking clue to the divine nature. We see that "the mills of God" do indeed "grind slowly" and "exceeding small" because of the *kind* of creativity that is God's, the infinite patience it takes, and his infinite willingness to take that patience. We see, as the greatest of the classic Christian theologians have seen, each in his own way, that God must be far greater than any of our human ways of talking about him, of looking at him, or defining him. To celebrate God in pantheistic terms as the All-in-all is as inadequate as to acclaim him in deistic or theistic terms as *ganz anders*, as "The Wholly Other." We can see the nature of God only in what we can see of his work, and the further we grow in the spiritual dimension the better the perspective we can obtain of the way he works. What we call "Nature," which is what scientists labor to understand, is an aspect of God in the sense that it represents one stage of his work; but it is by no means the final stage and certainly not the only one, although it seems to be basic to the structure of all his work. No model we can devise to describe God can possibly be adequate; but some are less misleading than others and none can be worth taking seriously that do not take into account and do justice to what can be perceived of the way he works. Orthodox Christians, who see Jesus Christ as the unique incarnation of God, point to the Person of Christ as the manifestation of God on earth and therefore point also to Christ's Work as the clue to God's nature.

Although God is entirely free, uninhibited by the action of anyone or anything external to himself, and unrestricted by the array of circumstances that limit and impede us, he must be able freely to restrict himself if he so chooses. Why should he so choose? Only through this gracious love constantly outpouring toward all that he is eternally creating could the making of such a choice ever arise. As I have suggested elsewhere,[1] God, being eternally engaged in a creative enterprise that entails self-sacrificial love, is *by his nature* not only beyond and within us but also self-limiting. That is to say, in the act of creation he so involves himself in his creature that he not only lets his creature *go*; he lets his creature *be*, giving the creature freedom to develop, to grow, to evolve, gradually winning such freedom as the creature can attain by independent struggle, yet making available to that creature at every step in the evolutionary process an incalculably rich treasury of spiritual nourishment and help. The help cannot be thrown at the creature; nor can it be fed into the creature as if by an

1. *He Who Lets Us Be* (New York: Seabury Press, 1975).

intravenous injection, for even God can no more force help
upon anyone who does not in some way seek and ask for it
than can one help an alcoholic before he chooses to seek
help. Hence the Gospel injunction (Matthew 7.7) to ask and
to seek and the promise that by so doing you will receive and
find. Hence likewise the Deuteronomic promise (Deuterono-
my 4.29): "But you will seek Yahweh your God from there,
and if you seek him with all your heart and with all your soul,
you shall find him." So it is that divine Being can surround
us with and immerse us in his love while at the same time
according us and all his creatures whatever spiritual independence we have won.

So it is not merely that I reap what I sow; my life is part of a
far greater pilgrimage. What I do or fail to do has inevitable
consequences for me and so for others. According to the
evolutionary principle, I am growing. I have it in my power to
stunt that growth or to promote it. Moreover, all that I do I do
in the presence of the divine action that is antecedent to all
else and that continues to operate in the present moment. The
contemplation of all this leads me directly to the adoration
of the divine Being who is the source of it all and to whom I
owe existence: the most precious of all gifts because it is the
condition of all else.

Mystical encounter with God seems no longer, then, a
strange, deviant phenomenon but is directly related to the
precious stuff of daily life: that which makes life superlatively
worth living. There is a long way ahead of me and I shall need
rest before going on to the next stage of my pilgrimage; but
with my consciousness raised to its present level and in the
knowledge that it has unlimited possibilities, I am filled with
hope. Dangers lurk around me and ahead of me, but such is
my confidence that I know I shall not be destroyed. With the
same kind of assurance that the psalmist felt, I know that
angels shall bear me up in their hands (Psalm 91.12); nor is
this a mere pious hope but certain knowledge. With Mother
Julian of Norwich I know that I may "be tempested" but
also that I shall not "be overcome."

Mystical encounter with God, when genuine, is self-authenticating, because in it the soul transcends normal levels of consciousness. The only analogy the great mystics have to offer is that of human love and friendship. We all surely know the immense difference between genuine love and a spurious love that is really mere self-love. Inauthentic mysticism is in this respect much the same. Between such self-love and the genuine communion with divine Being that occurs when the soul is face to face with God in mystical encounter lies the kind of difference that is found between self-indulgent self-love and self-sacrificing love of another. There is no mistaking the one for the other when one has known both. The mystic has learned to walk with God as a friend and to accept the absolute ethical demands that God makes of his beloved.

For a soul to make this supreme discovery needs more preparation than could be accomplished in one little life. It requires long antecedent spiritual evolution. For the soul that has reached this stage has no ulterior selfish motive in seeking the mystical encounter. Such a soul has come to the point so well expressed by Newman in the soul's dialogue with the angel in *The Dream of Gerontius*:

> I would have nothing but to speak with thee
> For speaking's sake. I wish to hold with thee
> Conscious communion. . . .

12

Evolution and the "Blessed Assurance"

> *Yea, though I walk through the valley of the shadow*
> *of death, I will fear no evil; for thou art with me,*
> *thy rod and thy staff they comfort me.*
>
> Psalm 23 (KJV)

That the universe has an evolutionary character of some sort is very widely recognized by educated people today. The question is: what precisely are the modes of the evolution? Is there, for instance, any ground at all for what is celebrated in Christian thought as "the blessed assurance of the saints"? It is certainly not provided in the idea of natural selection; but we need not suppose that natural selection is the only mode of evolution that is at work in the universe.

We must recognize, however, that natural selection was the mode of evolution that, within a decade or so of the publication of Darwin's great work, was generally accepted by virtually every German, British, and American scientist. Herbert Spencer's "social Darwinism" came later and was also highly influential. In 1873, Whitelaw Reid, in an address at Dartmouth College, noted that "ten or fifteen years ago the staple subject here for reading and talk, outside study hours, was English poetry and fiction. Now it is English science. Herbert Spencer, John Stuart Mill, Huxley, Darwin, Tyndall, have usurped the places of Tennyson and Browning, and

Matthew Arnold and Dickens." Darwin's evolutionary theory, along with the critical study of biblical literature and the comparative study of the great religions of the world, had an enormous effect on people's attitude to traditional presentations of Christian faith. Henry Ward Beecher, probably the most prominent American preacher of his day, had already in the previous year warned the students at Yale Divinity School that if preachers failed to take such studies into account they would find themselves talking to empty pews. Such warnings were salutary: much needed and by some heeded. Unfortunately, while evolutionism was penetrating every aspect of intellectual life, its exponents did not always pay enough attention to distinguishing the different forms that it might take and their implications.

Intelligent preachers saw easily enough, for example, that the evolutionary principle could be seen in the Bible and that contemporary biblical scholars were showing that the Bible itself is in fact a literature that had been evolved over a period of at least a thousand years and had gone through complex editorial processes. Moreover, they recognized that thinkers such as Hegel and Comte, who had died before *The Origin of Species* had been published, had taught forms of evolutionism and that Spencer was adopting evolution as a universal principle to be applied to all phenomena. What they by no means always recognized was that the universal principle was based on a particular understanding of evolution and that a special method was being used in applying it. Spencer himself developed his evolutionary views gradually. At first he apparently meant only that the order of nature is the result of a gradual process and that this process entails some kind of progress. Eventually, however, he seems to have found a criterion of "higher" and "lower" progression and degeneration in the process that is independent of chance. In the end, in his preface to the last part of his *Ethics*, published in 1893, Spencer admitted that the concept of evolution had not "furnished guidance to the extent he had hoped."

No form of evolutionary theory, however, could have the kind of explanatory function he seems to have been seeking, without first postulating an intelligent and beneficent divine Being operating according to the karmic "law."

We recognize, from an elementary study of astronomy and physics, that everything has a life history. No star, including our own sun, can shine forever without change. Every star is actively radiating energy at an enormous rate into the depths of space. Either the energy in the star must be replenished or it must eventually cease to shine. There are young stars and old stars. Of course the age of a star is stupendous in comparison with the age of even the giant redwoods in California that were there before the time of Moses. Yet we must recognize that only the scale is different; the evolutionary principle is fundamentally the same. When God is seen as behind the whole process, the universality of the evolutionary principle becomes plain. It operates at many levels and in many modes, but it is universal.

Humanity is peculiarly interesting in this regard, not only because it is "where we are at" but also because it represents a dramatic change in the evolutionary pattern. It is as if the key and the tempo of music were suddenly to change and a new theme developed. There is a connection between the old music and the new, but the new partly leaves the old because it has something different to do that the old music by itself never could have done. We are at a crucial place in an evolutionary development: a place at which the human animal develops the capacity to grow up to a level of consciousness far beyond what we can now grasp. Our souls are in course of development; some younger, some older, all evolving. As at school and college, graduation from one stage to another is no more and no less than what it literally means: graduation (from *gradus*, a step) is stepping from one level to another, from one dimension to another dimension, from one kind of awareness to another kind. We may be highly developed by comparison with some within the sphere of humanity yet underdeveloped compared with others. What strikes each one of us more and more as we enter upon higher modes of consciousness is the sense that, come what may, all is well with us because we are, as Paul puts it (I Corinthians 3.9), "fellow workers with God." That is ground indeed for the "blessed assurance of the saints."

At the lower reaches of the evolutionary process biological entities are swept on and upward by the working of the process itself. The higher they go, the more awareness they develop, the more individual effort plays a part. In man this is notably the case. The biblical notion that man is made in the image of God is a way of affirming that man has a special capacity for creative spirituality that can make him an agent in the divine evolutionary process that is creation. The individual man or woman develops his or her individuality and goes on developing it through relationships of love. The further one so develops, the greater the role of one's own effort. With greater freedom come greater responsibilities. Paradoxically, so also comes deeper and deeper awareness of help from beyond. Equally fatal to progress, however, are exclusive reliance on the power beyond oneself, on the one hand, and, on the other, a smug satisfaction with one's own efforts.

At Yale Divinity School in 1959, at the opening of the academic year, Dr. William Muehl spoke of the "smug vulgarity that rises like a mist from the swamp of blessed assurance." He was indeed right in calling attention to the horrible caricature, so prevalent today, of the doctrine of "blessed assurance" that both consoled the heirs of the Reformation and filled them with a constancy that turned self-sacrifice into joy. For that doctrine, like all other religious teachings, was susceptible to corruption, and it has been indeed sadly vulgarized in popular Protestantism. But what precisely is the classic doctrine of "blessed assurance" and how was it understood by those in the past to whom it brought such special consolation and in whom it engendered such profound spiritual confidence?

The concept of "assurance" has deep biblical roots. In Isaiah 32.17 we read that "integrity will bring peace, justice give lasting security." What is asserted is that righteousness is its own reward in the sense that when one loves God and does one's best to do his will in leading a righteous life all fears and misgivings vanish, and one is so filled with the certainty of being forever in God's loving care that there can be no possible basis for fear, no matter what happens. The doctrine is strongly affirmed by the Reformation Fathers.[1] John Bunyan, in his *Grace Abounding*, tells us how the "assurance of God's love" came to him, filling him with comfort and hope, removing from him every personal fear. He saw his attitude as in line with that of Paul (Romans 8.38 f.): "For I am certain of this: neither death nor life, no angel, no prince, nothing that exists, nothing still to come, not any power, or height or depth, nor any created thing, can ever come between us and the love of God made visible in Christ Jesus our Lord." So, through my experience of the love of God, those terrors of hostile cosmic forces that continuously plague the average person in one way or another evaporate like moisture under a warm sun. In the ancient world fear of such forces induced an endless train of superstitious terrors, so that one's entire life was spent under the spell of fear. If it were not the evil eye that brought the foreboding, it would be something else, for such superstition feeds on itself: the little psychic irritations grow till they produce a cancer of the soul. The assurance of God's love destroys that pattern and so etches into the mind and heart confidence that the soul is permeated with a hitherto unknown and now enduring peace. John Bunyan relates that he was so taken with the love and mercy of God that he could not contain himself and would have waxed eloquent upon it "even to the very crows that sat on the ploughed land" before him, if they could have been able to understand him.

The classic Western theologians in the tradition of Augustine recognized the force of such ecstatic utterances and appreciated their spiritual meaning. Nevertheless, they generally took the view that, although such awareness of the implicates of God's love may very well come upon those who experience it (as no doubt had happened to themselves in many cases), such awareness, such heightened personal consciousness of personal assurance, is not to be taken as the criterion of whether a person has or has not been chosen by

1. See J. Calvin, *Institutes of the Christian Religion*, e.g., 1.17.7f.; 2.5.17; 3.2.14; 3.20.11f.; 3.20.47; 3.20.52; 3.24.7; 4.14.14; 4.17.29.

God. In short, we are not to judge the moral quality of a person's soul (one's being "in a state of grace," as the theologians would say) by the degree of ecstatic feeling he or she may have about it. What the classic theologians have been concerned to maintain here is akin to what we might say about the work of a mathematician, who *may* be ecstatic when he thinks he has solved a difficult problem but the quality of whose solution we would not judge by the degree of his ecstasy. Some people are temperamentally more phlegmatic than others, some more euphoric. One is not to determine the quality of a religious encounter by the shivers down one's back any more than one would measure the accuracy of an equation by the delight on the mathematician's face.

Yet when we have said all that it remains true that the profound sense of peace and certainty that nothing can injure me does tend to ensue from a deep awareness of the love of God. This is at the very root of the Christian Gospel. The Reformers, believing that the force of it had been lost through corrupt developments in Christian theory and practice in the late Middle Ages, greatly stressed this aspect of salvation. I am "snatched like a brand from the burning," saved, in Augustine's phrase, *inter pontem et fontem*, between the bridge and the river. Like the man in John 9, I can say, "whereas I was blind, now I see." Spiritual goodness and health irradiate me from within. That I should be filled with an overwhelming sense of peace and joy may not be strictly inevitable; but it is surely what is to be expected.

The "blessed assurance" of God's love and forgiveness and that all is well with my soul forever does not magically wipe out the consequences of sin. It does not alter the facts and it certainly does not mean that I need no longer grow; but it alters my relation to the facts and so delivers me from the fate of having my destiny determined only by these facts. When an alcoholic resolves by the grace of God to change his ways and to receive the assurance of God's forgiving love, his incipient cirrhosis of the liver is not suddenly eliminated and his body made completely healthy in the moment of his acceptance of grace. Nor are the karmic consequences of any of my evil acts or thoughts instantaneously removed. When you allow your room to get into such a mess that you decide to do something about it, the room does not tidy and clean itself; but such is your new attitude that you undertake the work and with joyful zest, which makes all the difference, since otherwise you would have gone on from bad to worse in the muck of your own making. The assurance I enjoy is not that God has let me off the hook by putting in order everything that I have abused or destroyed; it is, rather, that since I am now "right with God" I have the courage and the strength to put things right in my own life, no matter how long it takes. If I were paralyzed and you cured me, I would not grumble at the exercises I had to do in order to regain the full use of my limbs and so undo the damage of the paralysis; on the contrary, I would rejoice that by doing the exercises I could eventually walk and even run as much as I wanted. All this is eminently consistent with classic expositions of Christian doctrine, Catholic and Protestant. In Catholic tradition it has been notably stressed.

Its relevance to the concept of evolution is easily shown. If creation is through evolutionary means, an immense part of the process is realized through the acts of the evolving creature, within the general purpose of God. Yet such creative evolution does not preclude special divine acts of creation in the course of the general evolutionary movement. God is not the prisoner of his own methods. Evolution is growth, but growth does not preclude implanting. Such special activity of God within the evolutionary process might take many forms; it might be thus, indeed, that the mysterious "leaps" in the evolutionary process have been accomplished. Be that as it may, the recipients of divine grace are made aware that divine intervention has "saved" them as they were bound for the wrong track and that it has made possible their redemption, their spiritual renewal. In seeing the effect of this intervention in the stream of their lives, Christians become conscious of God as their friend. That their knowledge of his abiding love should bestow upon them the certainty that all is forever well with them is not surprising. This is the "blessed assurance" that is stressed in traditional expositions of Protestant orthodoxy and set forth in the standard old textbooks.

God's method in the conduct of the universe is uniform in the sense that it expresses the divine intent. In the earlier stages of creation it is expressed in what we call Nature, which is therefore in that sense an *aspect* of God. In Nature we experience a certain uniformity on which we can rely. In human consciousness we find no less the certainty of moral consequences, through karmic law. As the "laws of Nature" turn out to be more wonderful than at first they look, so the karmic principle unfolds itself as more gracious than at first it may appear. The evidence of the operation of the moral law may dawn more slowly on the human mind, since it does not appeal to the senses as does the natural order; but it is none the less seen in the long run to be just as certain and ineluctable as is the order we call Nature. The entire method, however, is evolutionary, gradual, progressive, operating from within the process of creation. It involves a continuous process of enfolding and unfolding, of growth and ripening, of disintegration and decay, followed by recurrence of the entire movement. Change is continuous. The time the process takes is by any reckoning immense: so vast indeed that it boggles our imagination. Yet more startling, more impressive, than the immensity of this time, more overwhelming than the trillions of galaxies of stars and their satellite planets and subsatellite moons, and more awesome than the stupendous intricacy of the submicroscopic, are the occasional divine interventions that Christians call grace, which come like showers of rain on the parched ground of our own negligence. In all this God is the indwelling force.

We ought to take note here, if only in passing, that for certain theological reasons Christian tradition has resisted the notion that God is eternally engaged in creation. Aristotle held that creation is eternal and, because he was for the Middle Ages the highest authority in what we would nowadays call the natural sciences, his opinion on this question seemed a challenge to Christian belief. Thomas Aquinas taught that from a rational standpoint Aristotle was right, for that is what would seem to be philosophically the inescapable conclusion; nevertheless, Thomas held, since the Bible reveals otherwise, Christians must accept the divine revelation as set forth in the opening passage in Genesis. I think, however, that Thomas, like many others, was wrong in this biblical interpretation, for in the Hebrew original it is far from clear, to say the least, that the notion of an eternal, ongoing creation is repudiated. If God is by his nature creative, then it is difficult to see how his creativity can ever stop. The notion that time was when God was quite happy sitting in heaven, so to speak, but suddenly thought it would be a good idea to create a universe, is plainly absurd.

Modern astronomers are divided on whether the universe is the result of a "big bang" or is eternal. I see no reason why it might not be both; that is, the universe as we know it might be the result of a vast explosion and also come to an end, only to be succeeded by another "big bang" such as that with which had begun the "last round." Needless to say, this is a highly speculative proposal. It would not only seem reasonable, however; it would accord with what the New Testament and other early Christian writers talk about when they allude to "the end of the age." This is the characteristic New Testament idiom: not "the end of the cosmos" or "the end of the world" but "the end of the age."

Some Christians have felt that although the evolutionary account of origins might hold true of the human body as of other biological entities, there must be some special creation to account for the development of the human soul. Indeed, that cannot be ruled out. Nevertheless, from what we know of the lower processes of creation, it does seem improbable. Some may think (I would say jejunely) that there is no need to postulate God at all in the production of the perpetual travail of creation. It seems to me, however, that if in that travail we find the presence of God at any point, it assures us of his presence all along. If you believe that you see the hand of God at any point in history, it is more than somewhat unlikely that his hand should be absent a thousand years thereafter.

What an evolutionary understanding of creation does point to, however, is something that turns out to be in fact very biblical. It is difficult on an evolutionary view of the universe to suppose that any animal, for example man, is intrinsically immortal. There are so many accidents in the course of the evolutionary process that result in annihilation, to say nothing of death from natural causes. On an evolutionary understanding of the universe, why should human beings have any special exemption from the universal principle of the creative process? All growth entails accident and may end in annihilation. May it not rather be, as I have so often argued elsewhere, that immortality is an achievement, made possible not only by one's own effort but by divine intervention, the conferring on one of a special opportunity, as a result of which one emerges in confidence of God's intent to invest one with the possibility of eternal life? Far from making me smugly assured of it in such a way as to cause me to loll in cozy self-satisfaction at my expected immortality, I am stimulated to work harder than ever to fulfill the capacity of which, through divine grace, I have now become aware.

The doctrine that man, as "an immortal soul," can never be annihilated is not only consonant with theosophical tradition; it is one of the several strands in the very confused Christian tradition on the afterlife. Nevertheless, the concept of conditional immortality accords with the teaching of Paul that while the "wages of sin is death," eternal life is a gift of God (Romans 6.23), in the receiving of which the recipient is made aware of his or her having been so favored that the sense of "blessed assurance" ensues. Sorely afflicted though he may be, he knows that his destiny is assured, that no tribulation or distress or persecution or other trouble can permanently hurt; indeed that "neither death, nor life, nor angels, nor principalities, nor powers, nor things present, nor things to come, nor height nor depth, nor any other creature, shall be able to separate us from the love of God" (Romans 8.35-39). Without some such confidence, express or implied, a Christian life would be meaningless. Even, however, if we insist on the "absolute" immortality of the individual self, the doctrine of assurance retains a meaning and a centrality.

Without an evolutionary concept of creation, this doctrine of "blessed assurance" is at best artificial, since it entails a seemingly arbitrary election by God of x and his noninvitation of y. In the evolutionary schema the election of x is not arbitrary since it emerges from karmic consequences and in, with, and through the evolutionary process; nevertheless it is still the expression of the unique love that is at the heart of God. (Christian theologians will note that this is a way of saying that both the view of Pelagius and the testimony of Augustine are justified in the proposal I make. Salvation is indeed the free gift of God, yet it is bestowed within an evolutionary process in which the human will is continuously operating. The classic distinction in Christian theology between election and freedom of the will has been generally misrepresented and widely misunderstood. It has been typically seen as an insoluble paradox: on the one hand, an omnipotent and omniscient God; on the other, his creatures endowed with freedom but so fallen that they are incapable of effectively using their will for their own salvation. On the contrary, it is paradoxical only in the sense in which Being itself is paradoxical. It is the paradox of love.

What makes it seem paradoxical is the nature of divine Being as gracious and loving, in short, the nature of the divine love, in which we participate, however meagerly it may be. In our workaday attitude to life and the world around us, we commonly expect nothing more of things and even of persons than that they should be *there*. That is because we think of Being in terms of bare existence. To the extent, however, that we perceive God at work, we know that his Being is gracious and loving and that this unique graciousness and love are growing within all beings that participate in him. They are seminally present in all that is in the evolutionary process: the smallest sparrow, even the leaves on the tree and the sand on the seashore; but in certain men and women they have begun to shine with resplendent light. An understanding of the evolutionary nature of all things, with God as the inner principle, the fount of their being and of their growth, helps very much to stimulate an awareness of the operation of that graciousness and of that love and of their centrality to the workings of the process.

Lack of understanding of the evolutionary nature of creation has vitiated Christian thought until a century or so ago. In unenlightened circles it still does. That is not to say that it has ever totally blinded everyone to the nature of God or to his redemptive work. Of course not. These are unfolded in Scripture and enshrined within the teachings of the Church. Evolution enables us, however, to make infinitely more sense of the ancient affirmations of faith than was formerly the case. It notably enhances our understanding of the nature of mystical experience and it strikingly illumines the doctrine of "blessed assurance" that has been so closely tied to Evangelical Protestant theologies.

The consequences of evolution for a Christian theology are much more far-reaching than even those that attended the teachings of Copernicus, the father of modern astronomy. For important as is the recognition that the sun, not the earth, is the center of our solar system, that is, after all, largely a matter of physics and chemistry. The evolutionary principle affects every aspect of creative growth. Once it is discerned at the spiritual level along with the karmic principle, its universality and pervasiveness come to be seen more and more clearly as the basis of our "blessed assurance."

13

Karma, Evolution, and Destiny

> *To have the sense of the eternal in life is a short flight*
> *for the soul. To have had it is the soul's vitality.*
> George Meredith, *Diana of the Crossways*

Our primary purpose throughout this study has been to show that recognition of the karmic principle, as a spiritual interpretation of that which lies behind the evolutionary universe of modern scientific thought, not only provides an intellectually plausible view but can be squared with basic Christian teachings. Moreover, we have seen that karma can be more easily understood in the light of what we now know of the evolutionary character of the universe. We have also taken note of the influence of thinkers, Protestant and Catholic, in showing how evolutionary concepts can enrich rather than impoverish our understanding of the Bible no less than that of the Scriptures of other religions.

We must recognize too, however, that while evolutionism has been widely, if sometimes reluctantly, accepted by thoughtful and educated Christians, we are not to expect everybody to accept the interpretation of it that is proposed in this book. Many people do not see in their lives any purpose of the kind that religious people acknowledge and celebrate. When no *such* purpose can be seen in one's own life, one is unlikely to see it elsewhere. Evolution may then be understood by such people in nihilistic, dysteleological ways, with humanity as purposeless as the rest of the universe. That is to say, if you should decline to acknowledge any sense of a purpose in your life such as religious people see in theirs, no assent-compelling theorem exists that could force you to accept an interpretation such as mine in the way that you could be forced to see that every triangle must contain two right angles. I could no more compel your acceptance than I could force you to see that life is worth living if you had decided that it is not.

There are nevertheless some strong pointers to the reality of the karmic principle. If we see even a glimmer of purpose in our lives and can go on to see them as unfolding to us a wider purpose, we must surely ask what lies behind the evolutionary process that invests it with any such purpose, and we will surely also wonder on what principle the process works. The glib answer traditionally provided in the Judaeo-Christian tradition is that God is working his purposes out. Before people were able to think in evolutionary terms, that was indeed pretty much all that could be said. If, however, we see the evolutionary character of all things and are willing to recognize any spiritual movement in the evolutionary process, we shall surely ask what might be the principle of its working. If evolution can be seen as "God's way of doing things," surely we must wonder on what principle he does them. If God be both righteous and loving he cannot work arbitrarily or capriciously. May not karma, then, be the principle that is to be sought?

I suggest that at least that is how we ought to put the question. After all, one can never discover more than one's questioning permits one to find out. If there be an evolutionary process at all, then (whatever it may portend for human and individual destiny) it must surely be a universal principle. Moreover, evolution is a knowledge-process in the sense that with our awareness of our own evolutionary self-unfolding comes an enhancement of our own self-knowledge. Although the tooth-and-claw survival view of the evolutionary process that led to the emergence of man might seem a plausible interpretation of what "natural selection" means, it becomes singularly implausible as a vision of how evolution might lead humanity to higher levels. For we all know that, even apart from anything that religious people may say about how we ought to behave, human selfishness and greed are self-destructive. They can lead to the annihilation of humanity, and under conditions now prevailing they are likely, if unchecked, to do so. At first glance, then, it would seem that if there be evolution at the human level at all, it must follow a very different pattern from whatever governs the natural-selection evolution at pre-human levels. How, then, can we talk of karma as a *universal* principle?

Here we must make some linguistic distinctions. In talking of "evolution," biologists and other scientists usually exclude the notion of intentionality, as do psychologists and sociologists when they talk of "behavior." Evolution need not mean development, nor need behavior mean conscious action. Here, then, is the nub of the problem. The biologists, in their professional capacity at any rate, are interested in how forms of life behave, not in moral or intentional acts such as constitute (or ought to constitute) the focus of religious people's concern. So we tend to get from them an account of the pre-human stages of evolution based on an understanding of evolution that excludes such ethical questions. But many psychologists and sociologists, when they give their accounts of human behavior, exclude from them no less the ethical motivations that interest religious people. So the distinction may not really lie between human and prehuman levels of an evolutionary process so much as between two different approaches, each having its own proper concern, perception, and focus: the one an empirical, scientific, morally neutral approach; the other an approach centered on moral and spiritual values.

More altruism is to be found at lower levels of evolution than was appreciated by some of the early exponents of evolutionism who painted a picture that came across to many as one of entirely amoral behavior at that stage of the process.

Even under a natural-selection view, however, selection favors altruistic conduct in those cases where some reciprocal benefit can be perceived. Such a reciprocity cannot but generate at least some primitive form of ethical concern. In the behavior of primates and cetaceans such as dolphins can be found much evidence for such reciprocal relationships, suggesting that something such as the moral aspect of the karmic principle operates, in however primitive a way, all through the evolutionary process. The extent, if any, to which self-conscious moral choices are entertained in lower forms of life is, however, questionable. In many humans, indeed, it is still underdeveloped, although in others it is deeply and inextricably rooted, with impressive spiritual consequences. Such reflections enhance the plausibility of the notion of karma.

As we have abundantly seen, however, karma is very much more than its ethical aspect. It entails a grander, metaphysical principle of balance and harmony that may be seen as the expression of divine Being or, more poetically, the very Voice of God. Although this all-encompassing karmic principle, including its ethical aspect, must be universal if it is at all what it is represented to be, we should not expect to find it *manifesting* itself equally through every stage of the evolutionary process. We ought no more to expect this than we expect the spirit of creative scholarship and original research to run equally through every stage of our educational system, manifesting itself in grade school and even kindergarten as much as in graduate school and postdoctoral investigations. We do find, however, embryonic forms of ethical concern that may have no less right to be so called than does much of what passes for this at the human level. The motherly care that many animals show for their offspring and the sense of family ties that encourage at least some form of altruistic reciprocity may be written off, if one be so disposed, as disguised egoism; but so, if one were to follow the teachings of Ayn Rand and others, might be the human counterparts of such animal behavior. True the sense of kinship we find and may applaud in some pre-human conduct is far from the highest and best kind we know; but then early forms of ethical awareness among human beings also fall far short of the highest standards we find among exceptionally noble men and women.

In the history of Israel we can see first how primitive was the tribe's ethical concern when it was merely struggling to survive yet seeing its struggle in religious terms. We can then look at Israel's struggles in achieving nationhood, and finally compare both with the highly developed ethical standards preached by the nation's prophets. Among these we find emphasis on the universality of judgment and righteousness. Yahweh becomes the Lord not only of the Hebrews but of all the earth, ready to judge his chosen people by the same standard by which he judges the other nations. If we can recognize as ethical these early stirrings of moral concern in primitive human societies, why not in more primitive societies still: the pre-human forms of life? Unless we can do something of this sort, what we noted in our chapter on our kinship with other forms of life must become very hollow talk indeed. Only if there is some continuity with what we reverence as moral awareness at our own level can we find any solid basis for invoking the reverence-for-life view that Schweitzer expounded and that is so widely approved among educated people today.

Ecologists talk much of the "balance of nature," which in earlier stages of the development of our planet, before agriculture began some ten thousand years ago, must have been fairly constant. We have in some ways radically changed our environment. Cattle in developed countries grow twice as fast as those kept by primitive tribes, while wheat fields in America yield several times as much per acre as do unimproved varieties. Are we to suppose, then, that we earthbound humans can really interfere with the karmic principle that lies behind our every thought and action no less than behind other issues such as the ecological balance of our planet? Of course not. We can change the ecology of our planet for good or ill only as we can change ourselves for good or ill, all within the operation of the karmic "law," which runs not only through the evolution of life, as biologists understand life, but through all creation. Shakespeare, in a striking echo of the Ancient Wisdom, captures the sense of that harmony that lies in the karmic principle when he puts on the lips of Lorenzo the beautiful words addressed to Jessica:

> How sweet the moonlight sleeps upon this bank!
> Here will we sit, and let the sounds of music
> Creep in our ears: soft stillness and the night
> Become the touches of sweet harmony.
> Sit, Jessica. Look, how the floor of heaven
> Is thick inlaid with patines of bright gold:
> There's not the smallest orb which thou behold'st
> But in his motion like an angel sings,
> Still quiring to the young-eyed cherubins, —
> Such harmony is in immortal souls;
> But whilst this muddy vesture of decay
> Doth grossly close it in, we cannot hear it.[1]

Evolution is an unfolding of that "sweet harmony" that is in divine Being itself and therefore in some way in all that is outpoured by that Being. Biological evolution represents but one aspect, however important, of a universal principle. That principle is what the Indian thinkers long ago identified as karma. At our stage of development, the most striking fruit of our awareness of the karmic principle is our consciousness of opportunity: opportunity provided through the operation of karma to work within the interstices it provides, however narrow and restricted these interstices may be. The concept of evolution, in its most general sense, alludes to any process of growth and development. We grow and develop in a vast variety of ways and as we do so our moral judgments acquire a larger perspective as well as a better set of criteria by which to evaluate them. Piaget, as a result of his studies of children from six years of age to twelve, felt able to distinguish an immense moral development within that period. Among people who continue an active development of moral and spiritual growth, however, we can find an even greater enhancement of moral perspective and spiritual awareness.

1. Shakespeare, *The Merchant of Venice*, Act 5, Scene 1.

Although we are far from appropriating the harmony at the core of all things, we do occasionally catch glimpses of it in those glorious moments of mystical vision that come to all of us as we make progress in the spiritual path. For the most part we struggle through a maze of discord and strife. Even in the struggle, however, we may remember how much better off we are than those at lower levels who cannot discern as we can even the possibility of purpose. We find, as we go on, that opportunity (that offspring of karma) knocks at our doors in strange and unexpected ways as we learn to extricate ourselves, at least in some measure, from the burden of karma. This opportunity knocks at most unforeseen times and in most unexpected places, enabling us through our response to see in it the very unfolding of God, a revelation of the majesty and beauty of the divine nature, which comes to us often, not to say usually, in a joyous and awesome surprise.

One's karmic destiny is governed by one's use of the opportunities karma affords. This entails, besides much else, the renunciation of egoism and the overcoming of self-centeredness. Paradoxically, although the development of altruistic attitudes is essential to my spiritual progress, such development leads to an intensification of my individuality. So important is this point for our summing up of the relation between the karmic principle and the evolutionary process that something must be said on it here. I shall allude to the writings of two very different but both deeply religious thinkers: Teilhard and Kierkegaard. I ask the reader's patience as we make this final exercise before drawing our study to a close.

Teilhard, in his repudiation of what he accounts an "other-worldly" strain in Christianity, ends by doing less than justice to the value of the individual. When he says that the true ego grows in inverse proportion to egoism, of course no spiritually-minded person can fail to concur. Self-centeredness of any kind is fatal to any kind of spiritual development. Teilhard, however, regards the "other-worldly" strain in Christian thought and practice as an "oriental" way of escape from reality. He says that there are at present two opposed

Christianities: (1) a Christianity that disdains the world (the way of escape) and (2) a Christianity that overcomes the world (the evolutionary way).² He eventually presents us with a vision of the future of man in which the second way (the one he approves) is achieved through a form of collectivization.

Now of course all religion has an "other-worldly" element and all genuine mystical experience presupposes a long evolutionary history, an incalculably long history of "overcoming." This is a commonplace of the Ancient Wisdom. The "other-worldly" element is as essential to spiritual growth as is the struggle in the arena of social conflict and is indeed inseparable from it. In the vision of the writer of the Apocalypse, the redeemed are portrayed as dressed in white robes with the palms of victory in their hands, for, we are told, they have "come through great persecution" (Revelation 7.9-17). What the writer indubitably had primarily in mind, however, was the persecution of Christians under Nero, which was due more than anything else to their "other-worldly" refusal to enter into the stream of the life of the Roman Empire by paying public homage to the State deities. They accepted cruel suffering rather than show even formal recognition of that which bound together the collectivized society: the Imperial Throne. To have done so would have been a renunciation of the priceless individual salvation they believed themselves to have won through Christ, for in their eyes the worship of the Emperor as a god was blasphemy. To have participated in it at all, even by a token libation of wine or pinch of incense at its altar, would have been a betrayal of him who had won them their individual salvation and had warned them against "the world," telling them on the eve of his crucifixion: "In the world you will have trouble, but be brave: I have conquered the world" (John 16.33).

Jesus, who claims this conquest, sets the world in opposition to himself, his disciples, and the work they are called to do. "If you belonged to the world," he tells them, "the world would love you as its own; but because you do not belong to the world,

2. Letter dated 1951, quoted in Claude Cuénot, *Pierre Teilhard de Chardin. Les grandes étapes de son évolution* (Paris: Plon, 1958), p. 316.

because my choice withdrew you from the world, therefore the world hates you" (John 15.19). The Spirit of God is at war with the world as it is at war with the Devil and the flesh, all three of which are renounced by the Christian at baptism. The overcoming or conquest of the world is a long warfare and the war is waged with the weaponry of the Spirit. The weapons against "the Sovereignties and Powers who originate the darkness in this world" (Ephesians 6.12) are carefully enumerated (Ephesians 14.17). So while the battle is fought on the terrain of the world, the flesh, and the Devil, it is fought against them.

Teilhard is, of course, not unaware of this element in the evolutionary process as he sees it; nevertheless, he is perhaps misled by his own bright vision into underestimating those forces in the world that mimic spiritualization as a cancer mimics the behavior of healthy cells in such a way as eventually to destroy them. That we must love all those who are moving toward the spiritualization of matter, by whatever way they are doing so, is beyond dispute. "Anyone who says, 'I love God,' and hates his brother, is a liar, since a man who does not love the brother that he can see cannot love God whom he has never seen" (I John 4.20). Nevertheless, as the same writer observes (I John 5.19), "the whole world lies in the power of the Evil One," who according to biblical teaching disguises his aims and camouflages his presence to make it seem as though he were on the side of the good angels. Similarly, collectivist enterprises that have as their aim some form of enslavement to political dictatorships can be made to sound like highminded and warmhearted adventures in spirituality when they are in fact in bitter combat against it. This is what Teilhard, despite his noble vision of the evolutionary character of spiritual development and the role of matter in its own transformation, seems to underestimate.

The value of the individual, like the value of novelty, was never fully or even well understood or appreciated until comparatively recent times. The first thinker in the West to give it serious attention was Duns Scotus in the late thirteenth century, with his doctrine of *haecceitas* (thisness); but the road from that perception to a full appreciation of the significance and value of individuality took many centuries. The ancients generally took the individual to be merely a copy or exemplar of the universal and therefore even at the best inferior to it. What is one chicken more or less compared to all the chickens in the world? Such an exaltation of the universal and the corresponding denigration of the particular was, broadly speaking, characteristic of all the great thinkers in the Western tradition from Plato to Hegel. Even the men of the Renaissance, although in their own way they perceived something of the importance of the individual, lacked the means of developing a serious philosophical theory of it. Escape from the long-standing presuppositions was difficult. Not till the nineteenth century do we find the beginnings of a radically fresh understanding of this question.

The first great thinker to express a new understanding of the spiritual value of the individual was Kierkegaard (1813-1855), which he did in his characteristically striking way. For Kierkegaard, God himself is "pure subjectivity." By this he means that divine Being itself preeminently encompasses the values we acclaim in the individual. This perception of the divine makes the reality of God more awesome, calling attention to God as the focus of the qualitative. Concern for the quantitative induces megalomania in one or other of its many forms. The qualitative is what spirituality is about.

Kierkegaard repeatedly insists that the category of the spirit is the single individual, while the category of the animal is the crowd.[3] He goes so far as to assert that in animal species the species is higher than the specimen (*Exemplaret*) and that only in humanity is the individual higher than the species.[4] In his characteristic style, he suggests that while wars and other calamities herd people together, plagues such as cholera have this advantage: they disperse people, teaching them by physical means that they are single individuals.[5] True Christianity does not join people together: it separates them

3. *Papirer.* Vol. XI^1 A370.
4. *Papirer.* Vol. XI^1 A485.
5. *Papirer.* Vol. XI^1 A506.

in order to unite the single individual with God. "And when a person has become such that he can belong to God. he has died away from that which joins men."[6] Kierkegaard, despite his ferocious attack on the Church, notably in his last writings, was by no means against the Church in so far as it succeeds in making people into single individuals. What he deplored was the tendency in the Church to exalt the institution, which then becomes a mere political unit giving people the illusion of spirituality while actually drawing them away from it. In his whimsical and hyperbolic way of preaching, he even questions whether the apostles were not already sliding into this trap at Pentecost when. according to the Book of Acts, they added three thousand to the Church through some sort of mass baptism. It would look, he says. as though they were pre-occupied with numerical extension (the larger the crowd the better) when in fact true spirituality is about intension, not extension.[7] " 'The single individual'—with this category the cause of Christianity stands or falls."[8]

Kierkegaard's insight into the relation between true individuality and spiritual growth was expressed in his very distinctive style. He thought of himself as a Christian Socrates. He had written his dissertation on the concept of irony in Socrates and he used satire polemically in an inimitable and highly effective way. He knew nothing about biological evolution: he died four years before Darwin's work appeared. With rare exceptions he was never out of the isolation of his native Denmark. The academic thought of his time and place was altogether inhospitable to ideas such as his. which, moreover, almost nobody listened to till about seventy years after his death when at last he began to be recognized as one of the greatest geniuses in human history.

There was certainly very little in the history of Western thought from which he might have borrowed. Yet he does recognize an ancestry for his ideas on individuality and the love of God in a certain tradition of Christian spirituality.

6. *Papirer.* Vol. XI[1] A96.

7. *Papirer.* Vol. XI[1] A189.

8. *Papirer.* Vol. VIII[1] A482.

He quotes Thomas à Kempis: "Every time I am with men I always come back less a man."[9] In the Stoics he could also find support. He quotes Seneca: "I come home again more niggardly, more arrogant, more sensual, more cruel, and more inhuman, because I have been among men."[10] Then he goes on to wonder: "To what a degree men would become men and lovable characters if they could be brought as single individuals before God."[11] While this sounds like a plea for an eremitical life, it is not at all so simplistic. It is Kierkegaard's way of saying that gregariousness and collectivity have nothing to do with the kind of relationship that makes possible that love out of which the individual develops.

In contrast to the process of natural selection that operates in biological development, our spiritual growth is advanced in much subtler ways that especially include the interchange of self-sacrificial love. Many of us perceive the import of this through devious ways in the course of the storms and stresses of human life. No doubt it takes many incarnations to learn even the rudiments of such spiritual evolution. Some of us have the advantage of being born into a family in which love is as fundamental to life as is the sense of the presence of God from early childhood. I remember, for instance, when I was a very small child, my mother telling me that any mother who was not ready to sacrifice her life for that of her child was, in her view, a monster. In accepting her view at the time as authoritative, I had at least a model of the kind of love out of which spiritual growth may issue. Yet one also learns from reaction to the selfishness that one meets in life. The Romans sometimes brought into the classroom a drunken oaf as a negative model to inculcate the virtue of temperance.

In mystical solitude alone with God we can learn much that no human company can teach us; nevertheless, at some stages of our development we need more than anything else the interaction of other people in creative, loving relationships. The Spirit of God leads us in this evolutionary process; but

9. Thomas à Kempis, *Imitation of Christ*, Book 1, Chapter 20.
10. Seneca, *Epistle* 7.
11. *Papirer*, Vol. X^1 A286.

we must appropriate the conditions needed for our growth. A tree or plant is programmed to absorb the rain and the sunshine that comes its way. We, by contrast, are given an often bewildering array of choices out of which we must select with no more than directional hints to guide us. Because of the complexity of our natures and the variety of our past actions, karma presents us with an increasingly great complexity, as we develop. No longer is it so much a question of a right path and a wrong one: it becomes more and more a choice among many right ones. Over the course of many lives we make many choices, learning in many ways in many kinds of human relationships the kind of love through which we grow. Sometimes, however, through deprivation of such loving relationships we learn to be alone with God, the source of that kind of love that makes us "single individuals."

We now come to a superlatively important point. Solitude with God could not have this function if God were *only* an objective reality permeating all things as oxygen permeates the air we breathe, as water surrounds us wherever we swim. For then we should be standing in no relationship when we left the haunts of men in order to company with God. Only because God is also pure subjectivity, confronting the individual from within his or her own soul, can that solitary companying with God play such a crucial role in our spiritual growth. Since God is pure subjectivity (whatever else he may be besides) he confronts us as individuals, recognizing the value of our individuality. So long as we have the moral strength to keep company with him in the solitude of our minds and hearts, we learn, however gradually, to be more and more individualized and therefore in some way more comfortable to the image of God that is our true nature and destiny.

Built into the higher reaches of the evolutionary process, then, is the unfolding of that kind of individuality that can be achieved only after an incalculably long time and as the result of innumerable human relationships. These relationships, entailing the growth of self-sacrificial love, so purify and strengthen the individual that he or she attains a more and

more distinctive individuality, coming closer and closer to
God who is superlatively and uniquely individual. It is indeed
the uniqueness of the individuality of God that so separates
him from all his creatures as to justify the strong emphasis,
in the Judaeo-Christian theological tradition, on the "Other-
ness" of God. We are, even the finest of us, only imperfectly
individualized. Angels and other beings who have attained a
higher mode of consciousness than we humans have so far
achieved must be more individualized still, becoming more
and more distinctive as they attain higher and higher spiritual
development. Divine Being, however, is unique and in his
uniqueness he respects the uniqueness of each individual and
so addresses his love to each individual as though there were
no other in all the universe.

What, then, is the destiny of man? As I work out my karma
and take the opportunities it affords, to what may I look
forward? In view of the role of and emphasis upon the individual and the concept of God as "pure subjectivity," it
might seem that our Western understanding of man's destiny
differs notably from the Eastern one as it is presented, for
instance, in basic Buddhist teaching. But is it really so? Let
us compare.

The Buddha taught that craving or desire is the enemy of
spiritual progress. There is, however, a remedy. Desire is, he
said, like a fire requiring fuel. Take away the fuel and the fire
wanes and dies. Meditation, the last point in the Noble
Eightfold Path, extinguishes the fire by focusing our awareness on something beyond desire. The goal of the practice of
meditation is Nirvana. This state is described as one that
transcends all opposites and so extinguishes the fires of
attachment. This theme certainly has counterparts in several
of the traditions of Christian mysticism. One need think only
of Nicholas of Cusa, for example, with his "coincidence of
opposites," and John of the Cross with his "Dark Night of
Sense" followed eventually by the "Dark Night of the Soul."
In Buddhism, however, is found a certain emphasis on the
notion of the extinction of the separate individual self. This
does not mean, as has too often been supposed in the West,

that nirvana is an extinction of existence. On the contrary, it is a collapse of all barriers to full existence. It is an extinction of the mind-constrictive fires of desire with all their self-delusion: yet it is a calm and golden enjoyment of reality far beyond our present imagining. It transcends personality and all the limitations attending it. Whatever was that Enlightenment that the Buddha claimed for himself and promised to his followers, it was not a diminution of existence, but, rather, an enrichment of it. Individuality is seen in terms of personality, which (as we have seen over and over again) is only a little less ephemeral than the color of our hair and the cast of our eyes. So of course its significance is belittled.

If we allow for differences in the ways in which East and West symbolize such concepts, it may be that the Buddhist vision of nirvana and the Catholic vision of heaven are less dissimilar than has been widely imagined in the West. The Catholic view certainly does provide for the intensification of individual awareness in the enjoyment of God: but the individual has been transmogrified by love: a love that has emptied him of all egoism and so fitted him to be united with God. This view of heaven is most vividly and beautifully developed and expressed by Thomas Aquinas in his concept of the nature of the Beatific Vision that constitutes the essence of the state of heavenly bliss. The Thomist account of future bliss is by far the most intelligible in Christian theology, which is notoriously confused in its treatment of the afterlife. According to Thomas, those who have attained the beatified state are portrayed as orbiting round the Being of God. Their enjoyment is cognitive: that is to say, the essence of the state consists in their enjoyment of knowing divine Being and of their relation to it. Their wills are engaged in the cognitive act; yet the delight is essentially a delight in *knowing* God. In this act of knowing they have thrown off all other joys as trivial and ephemeral. God alone has become sufficient. What can one lack when one has God? They have submerged all their other cravings and concerns. Yet in contrast to the Buddhist report their individuality, far from being burned away, is intensified. The more they love divine Being, the more they exhibit and develop their own individuality. They are as individual in relation to God as are Mercury and Jupiter in their relation to the sun they orbit.

The difference between these two reports is, I would submit, largely one of emphasis, reflecting an attachment to different modes of symbolization. By individuality the West does not mean personality, which by all accounts is in the long run as ephemeral and inconsequential as our hair and our toenails now seem to be. (One recalls how Teilhard, as a child, was impressed by the fact that he could have his nails and his hair cut and yet be his undiminished self.) Nor, certainly, does the East, when it talks of extinction, mean the extinction of existence but, rather, only of the cravings that limit the enjoyment of existence. So close, indeed, are the Buddhist and the Christian views of "heaven" that what is needed to understand them is not so much a bridge as a study of the way in which their respective symbols operate within their own systems.

All this is by no means to pretend that Buddhism and Christianity are merely two ways of saying the same thing. On the contrary, in many respects they are saying quite different things and this ought to be recognized by anyone who hopes to understand either. Nevertheless, in respect of their visions of the destiny of man, I would submit that they are much closer than is often supposed. Heaven and nirvana are described in very different idioms and with strikingly different emphases; but anyone who has seriously tried to understand what each is saying will end by seeing the two visions come into a common focus.

In the West, at any rate, the emphasis is clear: although the individual has many paraphernalia to discard and many trappings to throw away, he discovers as he disposes of them that his individuality, far from evanescing, is intensified. It is intensified because, paradoxically, it is the expression of that "pure subjectivity" that is divine Being. The closer the beatified spirit is to God, the more individual he is. As in Buddhism, so in Christianity: the consciousness is transformed. Of that neither side is in any doubt. The difference lies in the phenomenological description. The Stoic ideal is not far from

either. which is not surprising if one considers. on the one
hand. Stoic presuppositions about the divinity of the human
soul and. on the other. the immense influence of Stoic ethics
on early Christianity.

If, then, what we know of the workings of evolution in
biology and other "natural" sciences be interpreted in the
light of what we perceive of our relationship to divine Being
and of our expectation of the destiny that that relationship
entails, we shall see evolution as a principle permeating every
level of our experience. The karmic principle provides the key
to an understanding of how evolution must work at every level
and in every dimension of created being. According to this
principle all things do indeed work together for good. as Paul
affirms. although the process takes longer than the Western
world has generally understood. Yet everywhere in the world.
East or West. perceptive men and women have seen all this
in one way or another. Of course mystics and visionaries
have seen it; but so also even the common man. when he is
not completely in the grip of a literalistic understanding of
dogmatic teaching. has surely caught a glimpse of how things
are as he has repeated old proverbs such as "every dog has
its day." "God tempers the wind to the shorn lamb." "near
the Church. far from God." and "God's mill goes slowly. but
it grinds well." In these. no less than in the Ancient Wisdom
in the Sermon on the Mount. have been transmitted the great
truths about the life of the spirit: the deepest insight into our
own nature and the nature of Being itself.

Yet as with all knowledge of this kind. such truths do little
for us till we make them our own. allowing them to transform
our lives. Only then can we expect them to point us toward the
glorious life to come that is the destiny of all of us who have
learned. each in his or her own way. the secret of the ages.
Books and teachers guide us. focusing our eyes on the light
beyond us; but only the self-disclosure that comes from
making the knowledge our own can see us on the road that
leads us home.

Index of Persons

Abbott, Lyman (1835-1922), 21, 22

Alexander, Samuel (1859-1938), 16, 30

Anaximander, 17, 18

Aquinas, Thomas. See *Thomas Aquinas*

Aristotle, 3, 7, 15, 18, 99, 162, 177

Arnold, Matthew (1822-1888), 171

Augustine, 18, 19, 59, 60, 78, 81, 174, 175, 180

Baader, Franz Xaver von (1765-1841), 101

Beecher, Henry Ward (1813-1887), 171

Bergson, Henri (1859-1941), 28, 29, 30, 31, 161

Blavatsky, Helena Petrovna (1831-1891), 106

Boehme, Jakob (1575-1624), 101

Booth, William (1829-1912), 130

Bradford, John (c. 1510-1555), 60

Browning, Robert (1812-1889), 170

Bruno, Giordano (1548-1600), 98, 99, 100

Buffon, Georges Louis Leclerc, Comte de. See *Leclerc*

Bunyan, John (1628-1688), 60, 130, 174

Calvin, John (1509-1564), 81, 130, 174

Campbell, Joseph, 63

Carruth, William Herbert (1859-1924), 11

Cerminara, Gina, 44

Chesterton, Gilbert Keith (1874-1936), 118

Clement of Alexandria, 78, 83

Columbus, Christopher, 3

Comte, Auguste (1798-1857), 171

Copernicus, Nicholas (1473-1543), 2, 181

Cuénot, Claude, 189

Dante (1265-1321), 46, 116, 124, 166

Darwin, Charles (1809-1882), 1, 4, 5, 8, 11, 13, 15, 17, 19, 20, 23, 29, 30, 31, 35, 83, 95, 99, 100, 101, 160, 170, 171, 192

Darwin, Erasmus (1731-1802), 13

De Vries, Hugo (1848-1935), 31, 160

Dickens, Charles (1812-1870), 171

Drummond, Henry (1851-1897), 22, 23

Duns Scotus. See *Scotus*

Eckhart, (c. 1260-1327), 158

Einstein, Albert (1879-1955), 146

199

Other Quest Books on Karma and Evolution

BEING, EVOLUTION AND IMMORTALITY
By Haridas Chaudhuri

A disciple of Sri Aurobindo points up the value of the East's insights into the mystery of being when integrated with the Western world's awakening to the evolution of life.

CAYCE, KARMA AND REINCARNATION
By I. C. Sharma

The many parallels to be found in the Cayce philosophy and the ancient wisdom of India.

THE EVOLUTION OF INTEGRAL CONSCIOUSNESS
By Haridas Chaudhuri

The author bases his remarks on the disciplines of philosophy, history, education, science as he demonstrates the holistic nature of our consciousness.

THE BASIC IDEAS OF OCCULT WISDOM
By Anna Kennedy Winner

An overview of fundamental theosophic concepts including karma and evolution.

KARMA: THE UNIVERSAL LAW OF HARMONY
Ed. by V. Hanson & R. Stewart

Fourteen separate views on a subject that is increasingly interesting to Western readers. Authors include Dane Rudhyar, Geddes MacGregor, and Ralph Waldo Emerson.

Available from:
QUEST BOOKS
306 West Geneva Road
Wheaton, Illinois 60189